MW00366042

Varieties of
Christian Universalism

Varieties of Christian Universalism

EXPLORING FOUR VIEWS

EDITED BY
DAVID W. CONGDON

With contributions by
David W. Congdon, Tom Greggs,
Morwenna Ludlow, and Robin A. Parry

Baker Academic
a division of Baker Publishing Group
Grand Rapids, Michigan

Published by Baker Academic
a division of Baker Publishing Group
Grand Rapids, Michigan
www.bakeracademic.com

Printed in the United States of America

Library of Congress Cataloging-in-Publication Data
Names: Congdon, David W., editor. | Greggs, Tom. | Ludlow, Morwenna. | Parry, Robin A.
Title: Varieties of Christian universalism : exploring four views / edited by David W. Congdon ; with contributions by David W. Congdon, Tom Greggs, Morwenna Ludlow, and Robin A. Parry.
Description: Grand Rapids, Michigan : Baker Academic, a division of Baker Publishing Group, 2023. | Includes bibliographical references and indexes.
Identifiers: LCCN 2023018355 | ISBN 9780801095764 (paperback) | ISBN 9781540967121 (casebound) | ISBN 9781493444021 (ebook) | ISBN 9781493444038 (pdf)
Subjects: LCSH: Universalism.
Classification: LCC BX9941.3 .V37 2023 | DDC 289.1—dc23/eng/20230605
LC record available at https://lccn.loc.gov/2023018355

23   24   25   26   27   28   29   7   6   5   4   3   2   1

For all those who have proclaimed a wider hope,
even at the expense of their own livelihood

Contents

Acknowledgments

Every published book is a journey that has unexpected twists and turns along the way, and this one was certainly no exception. Unfortunately, the twists in this case involved losing my job and having to rebuild my life in a new city. As a result, a book that I had hoped to publish three years ago took quite a bit longer to bring to completion, and I am immensely grateful to my fellow contributors—Tom Greggs, Morwenna Ludlow, and Robin Parry—for their patience with me. The book also changed significantly during this time, and while the final product is not what I had in mind, it is ultimately a better work for having gone through this purgative process.

My thanks as well to the team at Baker Academic for their forbearance. This project originated with Dave Nelson, who was generous and understanding when the book encountered difficulties. My thanks to Jim Kinney for sticking with the project. Alexander DeMarco provided exceptional copyediting, and I am grateful for his help and his friendship.

Christian universalism may be growing in popularity these days, but it remains highly taboo in most Christian communities. Universalism may not be culturally explosive, the way issues pertaining to race, gender, and sexuality are, but with respect to the institutional church itself, the doctrine of universal salvation may be the ultimate heresy—the one that most threatens the networks of power and resources that depend on the church having a monopoly on the source of eternal salvation. For this reason, so many pastors, theologians, and other church leaders have found themselves excluded and marginalized from their former communities over this doctrine. It is depressingly fitting that those who proclaim a more generous gospel are suppressed by those who insist on an ever more ungenerous account of the faith. I dedicate this book to those who have steadfastly announced a wider hope, even at risk to themselves.

David W. Congdon

Introduction

David W. Congdon

Christian universalism is having a moment. To be sure, it has had its moments throughout Christian history, but in a relatively short period of time it has gone from a minority position quickly dismissed as heretical, if not unthinkable, to a genuine option within the theological landscape. To be more accurate, however, "universalism" should be "universalisms," and "option" should be "options." Christian universalism today is not one thing, even though it is often treated that way by critics. The purpose of this book is not to argue for universalism—many others have done so already—but to clarify the breadth of the views contained within the umbrella of "Christian universalism."

The Rise of Christian Universalism

It is no accident that Christian universalism became more mainstream when it did or that it has become so controversial today. The rise of universal salvation as a thinkable option within Western Christianity occurred over the past two centuries largely as the result of two developments. First, modernity—including the many scientific, philosophical, cultural, and political changes—created a crisis of ecclesiastical authority that opened up the possibility of religious autonomy, the idea of faith as a personal conviction independent of any institutional authorization. If salvation was not in fact determined by official church doctrine or ecclesiastical boundary-making, then the doors were open for rethinking the limits of redemption—and theologians like Friedrich Schleiermacher (1768–1834), whose universalism set the terms for subsequent liberal theology, exploited this opportunity. Second, the late eighteenth and nineteenth centuries, with expanding European colonialism and missionary movements, saw theologians and philosophers grapple with the reality of what became known as "world religions" and the problem of global religious pluralism. While theologians initially sought to ensure that Christianity remained the supreme and absolute religion, with all others as inferior and subordinate alternatives, that form of Christian supremacy became increasingly untenable. The growing awareness of religious pluralism and global diversity made many of Christianity's claims of exclusivity difficult to sustain both rationally and morally. As people have grown more disillusioned with the institutional church, universalism has become an attractive doctrinal option. For this very reason, though, universalism has become especially controversial in recent years, as church authorities grow anxious about the loss of members and the deviations from what is considered to be orthodox tradition.

While there were precursors, the mainstreaming of universal salvation arguably began with Karl Barth's proposal in *Church Dogmatics* II/2 (1942) for a universal election (which he denied was universalism—more on that later).[1] Barth's was a radically Christocentric theology that understood election exclusively in terms of Jesus Christ as the one elected for both glorification and

---

1. There were certainly many earlier proponents of Christian universalism, such as Schleiermacher or the Scottish author George MacDonald (1824–1905), but these could hardly be said to have brought universalism into mainstream theological conversation. In the twentieth century, Barth was preceded by the likes of Sergei Bulgakov (1871–1944), whose book *Bride of the Lamb* (1939) made a modern Orthodox case for universal salvation. But this work was not well known outside of Russian Orthodox circles for many years and was only translated into English in 2002.

condemnation, in whom all humankind is indirectly elected. In the process, he made his rejection of both double predestination and free-will salvation clear. Barth was such a significant theological figure, broadly respected on all sides of the theological and political spectrum, that he helped normalize ideas and positions that otherwise would not have received as much attention and respect. While he still rejected universalism—or at least regarded it as a position he could not take publicly—his arguments against eternal damnation and in favor of God's election of all people in Jesus Christ made it easy for those who followed him to take the next logical step.

The discussion about universalism continued with the publication of Bishop John A. T. Robinson's *In the End, God* in 1950—a response to his debate with Thomas F. Torrance over the matter. Robinson's book was ahead of his time and was later overshadowed by the controversy provoked by the publication of *Honest to God* in 1963. His earlier book, reprinted in a special edition in 2011, raised many of the crucial theological questions that would animate later works on this topic. In addition to his sophisticated analysis of New Testament eschatology, Robinson focused on the logical options available to Christians given the scriptural witness to two competing "myths of the end," the word "myth" referring to any model for which "direct evidence is unobtainable."[2] The first myth is universal salvation, the idea that God will be "all in all" (1 Cor. 15:28); the second myth is final separation. The question is how to hold these myths together.[3] The available options are the following:

- Calvinism (double predestination): God *will* be all in all *because* of the destruction of those whom God has rejected.

2. John A. T. Robinson, *In the End, God: A Study of the Christian Doctrine of the Last Things*, ed. Robin Parry, special edition (1950; repr., Eugene, OR: Cascade Books, 2011), 27.
3. Robinson, *In the End, God*, 93–95.

- Possibilism: God *may* be all in all, but the final result is up to humankind.[4]

- Traditional View: God *will* be all in all *despite* the destruction of many.

- Universalism: God *will* be all in all.

One of the most influential aspects of Robinson's book was his critique of the view I refer to here as possibilism, about which he said, "Of all positions, though it sounds the most humble, it is in fact that most subtly unbiblical. For the New Testament never says that God *may* be all in all, that Christ *may* draw all men unto himself, but that he *will*."[5] His analysis of the traditional view, represented in the book by Thomas Aquinas, criticizes the way love and justice are pitted against each other, as if these attributes could compete within the being of God. Robinson here follows a path previously pioneered by Barth, though he draws on Emil Brunner's work to make the point. "God is the eternal 'Yea,'" he argues, "and if his last word is any other than his first . . . then his love is defeated and he is not omnipotent."[6] Anything less than universalism, Robinson argues, involves a contradiction within God—an inability for God to be God.

Beginning in 1962, the Catholic theologian Karl Rahner began developing his concept of "anonymous Christianity" as a response to the challenge of religious pluralism that did not require abandoning his commitment to the doctrine that "outside of the church there is no salvation" (*extra ecclesiam nulla salus*).[7] Rahner's posi-

---

4. "Possibilism" is my term. Robinson calls this "Two Possible Futures."

5. Robinson, *In the End, God*, 96.

6. Robinson, *In the End, God*, 101.

7. See Karl Rahner, *Theological Investigations*, 23 vols. (New York: Crossroad, 1961–1992), 5:115–34 ("Christianity and the Non-Christian Religions"), 6:390–98 ("Anonymous Christians"), 12:161–78 ("Anonymous Christianity and the Missionary Task of the Church"), 14:280–94 ("Observations on the Problem of the 'Anonymous Christian'"), 17:39–50 ("Jesus Christ in the Non-Christian Religions"), 21:171–84 ("Christianity's Absolute Claim").

tion shifted the focus from the objective pole (Has God accomplished the redemption of all humanity?) to the subjective pole (Can a person be redeemed without consciously identifying with Christian faith?). Unlike Protestant approaches to universalism, Rahner's was grounded in a *ressourcement* metaphysics of creation that understood the natural human condition to be embedded in the gratuitousness of divine grace. Hans Urs von Balthasar was one of the sharpest Catholic critics of Rahner's account, and it was his 1986 work *Dare We Hope "That All Men Be Saved"?* that offered the next widely discussed approach to the question. Balthasar's view was not an advance but a restatement of the same dilemma that Robinson had pointed out over thirty years earlier—namely, that the Bible contains two sets of passages, universalist and particularist. Balthasar's "solution" to this was to argue that we cannot take a definitive position either way.[8]

John Hick took up the same set of questions that animated Rahner's work but developed a more definitive position. In a series of influential works, he increasingly built an argument for a religious pluralism that saw all religions as rooted in the same divine reality. As he put it in the title of his 1980 work, "God has many names," and Christianity provides one of those names. Though he was once a conservative evangelical, his work on the problem of evil led him to embrace universal salvation as the only coherent response to theodicy.[9] But his position changed again with his move "to Birmingham, with its large Muslim, Sikh and Hindu communities, as well as its older Jewish community." Here he began to recognize that, in these other religious gatherings, "essentially the same kind of thing is taking place . . . as in a Christian church—namely, human beings opening their minds to a higher

---

8. Hans Urs von Balthasar, *Dare We Hope "That All Men Be Saved"? With a Short Discourse on Hell*, trans. David Kipp and Lothar Krauth (San Francisco: Ignatius, 1988).

9. John Hick, *Evil and the God of Love* (London: Macmillan, 1966).

divine Reality."[10] Hick refused to accept that one must either deny the truth-claims of one's own religion or assign other religions to an inferior or subordinate position in the hierarchy of truth. In an effort to remain faithful both to his own faith and to the universe of other faiths, he developed the idea that doctrines like the incarnation are myths or metaphors for divine truths that transcend any particular religion.[11] The incarnation remains Christianity's unique way of describing a truth of the divine that other religions use different metaphors to convey.

Toward the end of the century, Jürgen Moltmann's work provoked fresh conversation thanks to the 1995 publication of *The Coming of God*, which included his mature argument for universal restoration—a position that suffuses his many works on eschatology.[12] Ever since his 1964 book *Theology of Hope*, Moltmann has presented a consistently eschatological account of theology rooted in a Reformed conviction that God will be faithful to God's promises.[13] For Moltmann, as a panentheist, the being of God is bound up with the destiny of God's creatures, so that the loss of anyone would call into question the constancy of God's love and our confidence in God's promises. Moltmann's work was also notable for the way it united the soteriological question of universalism with the emancipatory concerns of liberation theology. The universal horizon of God's redemptive grace is a thoroughly political horizon meant to provoke and sustain political action in view of God's coming reign.

The discussion took a turn on the eve of the new millennium when the philosopher Thomas Talbott published *The Inescapable*

10. John Hick, *God Has Many Names: Britain's New Religious Pluralism* (London: Macmillan, 1980), 5.

11. John Hick, *God and the Universe of Faiths: Essays in the Philosophy of Religion* (London: Macmillan, 1973), 16, 165–79.

12. Jürgen Moltmann, *The Coming of God: Christian Eschatology*, trans. Margaret Kohl (Minneapolis: Fortress, 1996).

13. Jürgen Moltmann, *Theology of Hope: On the Ground and the Implications of a Christian Eschatology*, trans. James W. Leitch (New York: Harper & Row, 1967).

Love of God (1999), a work that took a more philosophical approach to the subject. Talbott presented readers with three propositions that have a longstanding basis in the Christian tradition:

1. God's redemptive love extends to all human sinners equally in the sense that he sincerely wills or desires the redemption of each one of them.
2. Because no one can finally defeat God's redemptive love or resist it forever, God will triumph in the end and successfully accomplish the redemption of everyone whose redemption he sincerely wills or desires.
3. Some human sinners will never be redeemed but will instead be separated from God forever.[14]

Talbott's argument is that each of the traditional positions rejects one of these three propositions. Calvinism rejects 1, Arminianism rejects 2, and universalism rejects 3. Talbott's own position on universalism is what we might call an "evangelical" approach to universal salvation, meaning a version based on a plain reading of scripture that accepts the existence of hell while believing that hell is a means toward the greater end of complete redemption.[15] There were earlier evangelical accounts of universalism (as Robin Parry's chapter in this volume points out), but they had been largely if not entirely forgotten. When most twentieth-century theologians discussed the topic of universalism, the account was generally some version of the ancient Christian idea of *apokatastasis*, in which salvation is a restoration of the original cosmos rooted in the metaphysics of creation and the necessity of God's cosmic redemption. Talbott's evangelical approach assumed a more individual, post-Reformation understanding of salvation as a personal

14. Thomas Talbott, "Towards a Better Understanding of Universalism," in *Universal Salvation? The Current Debate*, ed. Robin A. Parry and Christopher H. Partridge (Grand Rapids: Eerdmans, 2003), 3–14, at 7.
15. Thomas Talbott, *The Inescapable Love of God* (Salem, OR: Universal Publishers, 1999).

response of faith to the gospel. While Talbott's approach was more logical, in keeping with his area of academic expertise, his work paved the way for Gregory MacDonald to publish *The Evangelical Universalist* in 2006, which added a more nuanced analysis of the relevant biblical texts to address the arguments that evangelicals were most likely to raise.[16]

Evangelicals were scandalized in 2011 when one of their most prominent young pastors, Rob Bell, published *Love Wins*, leading John Piper to tweet, "Farewell Rob Bell."[17] Bell's book did not take an explicitly universalist position but raised questions about traditional beliefs regarding exclusivism, hell, and eternal punishment. He suggested that many Christians could not take literally many of the doctrines that were officially taught. This was hardly the first time evangelicals had dealt with a controversy about the afterlife. John Stott sent shock waves through the global evangelical community in 1988, when he presented arguments against the traditional idea of eternal conscious torment and defended the doctrine of annihilationism (also known as conditionalism).[18] In 2004, megachurch pastor Carlton Pearson, at Higher Dimensions Family Church in Tulsa, Oklahoma, was labeled a heretic for his belief in universal reconciliation, leading to a widely heard episode of *This American Life* in December 2005 ("Heretics"), which eventually became the movie *Come Sunday* in 2018. The documentary *Hellbound?* (2012) featured Parry and Talbott, among others, and probed why Christians are so invested in the belief in hell.

In 2019, the American Orthodox theologian and public intellectual David Bentley Hart published *That All Shall Be Saved: Heaven, Hell, and Universal Salvation*, offering an argument for universal salvation rooted in the classical theism of Origen and

16. Gregory MacDonald, *The Evangelical Universalist* (Eugene, OR: Cascade Books, 2006). Gregory MacDonald is the pseudonym used by Robin Parry.
17. John Piper (@JohnPiper), Twitter, February 26, 2011, 3:09 p.m., https://twitter.com/johnpiper/status/41590656421863424?lang=en.
18. David L. Edwards and John R. W. Stott, *Evangelical Essentials: A Liberal-Evangelical Dialogue* (London: Hodder & Stoughton, 1988).

Gregory of Nyssa, as opposed to the more evangelical approaches of MacDonald and Talbott.[19] Hart's central argument for universal salvation is moral and metaphysical, rooted primarily in who God is rather than what God has done according to the Christian tradition: God cannot be the Good itself if any part of creation is consigned to hell. For any theology that makes hell a necessary feature, "the choice to worship God rather than the devil is at most a matter of prudence."[20] The appearance of Hart's work brought the resurgence and mainstreaming of universalism full circle. As a scholar whose traditionalist bona fides were unquestionable—having published many of his early articles in venues like *First Things*—the doctrine of universal salvation could not be dismissed as the work of theologians who were dismissive of the classic orthodox tradition.[21]

Before taking leave of this historical survey, it is impossible to ignore the exceedingly white and male nature of the universalism discourse. For feminist theologians like Rosemary Radford Ruether, this is hardly accidental. In her 1983 work *Sexism and God-Talk: Toward a Feminist Theology*, Ruether examines the sexism baked into Christian eschatology in general, including accounts of universal salvation. The eschatology of personal immortality, she points out, arose in conjunction with a patriarchal system of thought that viewed redemption as a spiritual escape from the messy reality of embodied life. Sin and redemption were

19. David Bentley Hart, *That All Shall Be Saved: Heaven, Hell, and Universal Salvation* (New Haven: Yale University Press, 2019).

20. Hart, *That All Shall Be Saved*, 76. Hart's other key argument focuses on what it means to be human and how the limits of our understanding and agency make the notion of any person "choosing hell" or "rejecting God" incomprehensible.

21. It is thus ironic that Hart's book was preceded the previous year by Michael J. McClymond, *The Devil's Redemption: A New History and Interpretation of Christian Universalism*, 2 vols. (Grand Rapids: Baker Academic, 2018), a work that set out to argue that universalism was fundamentally an esoteric, gnostic, heterodox tradition alien to classical orthodoxy. For Hart's review of McClymond, see David Bentley Hart, "'Gnosticism' and Universalism: A Review of 'The Devil's Redemption,'" *Eclectic Orthodoxy*, October 2, 2019, https://afkimel.wordpress.com/2019/10/02/gnosticism-and-universalism-a-review-of-the-devils-redemption/.

gendered by virtue of their association with carnality and spirituality, respectively, since women were reduced to the bodily task
of reproduction while men were given the task of rational inquiry
and theological discernment. Eschatological redemption, for early
Christians, meant the transformation of all human beings into
the male, spiritual body of the original creation. Ruether extends
her analysis from patriarchy to coloniality by drawing upon the
Indigenous scholar Vine Deloria Jr., who critiques Christianity's
salvation history narrative for its colonialist logic. For Deloria,
"the idea of a universal linear project of salvation through history, leading from creation and the saving acts of God in Israel
and Christ through the Church to the end of the world, trans-
lates into a universal imperialism."[22] Ruether goes on to reject all
Christian eschatologies that assume a personal afterlife because
of the imperialist logic of historical eschatology and the egotism
of individual immortality. She argues for a return to the Hebraic
emphasis on shaping "the beloved community on earth," as well
as an agnosticism about the afterlife.[23] My own chapter in this
volume—following my 2016 book, *The God Who Saves*—is an
effort to take seriously Ruether's critique of eschatology in a conception of universalism that does not have a conscious afterlife.

Mapping the Varieties of Universal Salvation

Reviewing this brief history of universalism over the past century
should make it apparent that universalism is not a single theological doctrine but more like an umbrella of theologies that share
certain features or driving questions. The key feature, framed
positively, is that God's salvation, however understood, ultimately
encompasses all people. It might be more accurate, however, to

22. Rosemary Radford Ruether, *Sexism and God-Talk: Toward a Feminist
Theology* (Boston: Beacon, 1983), 250. See Vine Deloria Jr., *God Is Red* (New York:
Grosset & Dunlap, 1973).
    23. Ruether, *Sexism and God-Talk*, 256.

frame this feature negatively—as the conviction that no one will be eternally punished in hell or destroyed or left irrevocably abandoned by God. Whatever else universalists believe, they tend to agree that no human beings are going to spend eternity in spiritual anguish. That aside, proponents of universal salvation differ greatly on how they arrive at this common ground, and even how they flesh out what that common ground looks like—hence the need for typologies to map out the various options.

Robin Parry and Christopher Partridge provide one such typology in their 2003 volume, *Universal Salvation? The Current Debate*.[24] They begin by distinguishing between three main categories of universalism within Christian theology: multiethnic, Arminian, and strong. The first two are not categories of universal salvation but simply theologies that refer to "all" people in some sense. Multiethnic universalism simply means that God calls people from every nation or people group to become followers of Jesus Christ, and thus no ethnic or racial group is excluded from the community of faith. Arminian universalism is their term for theologies that affirm the possibility in principle of universal salvation on the (actually impossible) condition that all individuals respond to the gospel in faith, in contrast to "Calvinist" theologies that deny the possibility of universal salvation on the grounds that some people are definitely rejected by God. In contrast to Calvinism, the Arminian position assumes that salvation is effective only when the individual consciously believes in Christ. In my earlier work, I call this position potential universalism in distinction from actual universalism, or what Parry and Partridge call strong universalism.

Parry and Partridge divide strong universalism into three subcategories: (a) non-Christian universalism, (b) pluralist universalism, and (c) Christian universalism. Non-Christian universalism

---

24. Robin A. Parry and Christopher H. Partridge, introduction to *Universal Salvation? The Current Debate*, ed. Robin A. Parry and Christopher H. Partridge (Grand Rapids: Eerdmans, 2003), xv–xxvii, at xv–xix.

refers to religious systems outside of Christianity that believe all people will reach the "ultimate good." Pluralist universalism refers to programs that supposedly sit ambiguously between Christianity and other religions, and the authors here refer to John Hick's work on religious pluralism. Finally, Christian universalism, for Parry and Partridge, refers to a "wide family of views" committed to "working within a Christian theological framework" by making the claim "that all individuals will be saved through the work of Christ." Published twenty years ago, this volume was an important early effort to show that "universalism is a belief compatible with orthodox Christianity."[25] This framing, while necessary for its largely American evangelical audience, left the boundaries around what constitutes "orthodox Christianity" relatively unexamined, though the intervening years—here Hart's work is particularly notable—have made the problem of what counts as authentic Christianity a more pressing and complicated matter.[26] Categorizing Hick as a pluralist universalist as opposed to a Christian universalist, for instance, runs into problems of its own—not least of which is the fact that Hick himself speaks from a specifically Christian perspective and grounds his account of pluralist universalism in a metaphorical reading of God's incarnation in Christ. Indeed, it is hard to see much difference between Hick and Hart on these matters, especially when the latter, following the lead of early Christian theologians, develops his account of universalism largely in terms of a classical theism that is not exclusively Christian, as Hart demonstrates in his earlier work, *The Experience of God.*[27] Parry and Partridge themselves acknowledge that Christian universalists often "were motivated by a mixture of Christian and

25. Parry and Partridge, introduction to *Universal Salvation?*, xvii–xviii.
26. See David Bentley Hart, *Tradition and Apocalypse: An Essay on the Future of Christian Belief* (Grand Rapids: Baker Academic, 2022).
27. See David Bentley Hart, *The Experience of God: Being, Consciousness, Bliss* (New Haven: Yale University Press, 2013).

non-Christian philosophical ideas."[28] Attempting to parse what is Christian and what is not is an impossible task when Christianity has been a syncretistic, hybrid affair from the start.

For this reason, in my previous work *The God Who Saves*, I sought to move away from the "Christian" and "(non-Christian) pluralist" framing and toward a typology that analyzes Christian universalism according to the key distinguishing questions.[29] The two factors I used were the agent of salvation (the "who") and the temporal location of salvation (the "when"). The agent is the one who actualizes salvation, the one responsible for realizing redemption—however redemption, or salvation, is defined. The two relevant agents are God and the human person. I referred to universalism that takes God to be the agent of salvation as theo-actualism; and I referred to universalism that takes the human person to be the agent of salvation as anthropoactualism. Identifying the human person as the saving agent is not meant to suggest some kind of Pelagianism but simply indicates whose action is decisive. The two temporal locations for when salvation may be thought to occur are "in the past" (either a temporal past or an eternal past, i.e., always) and "in the present or future"—options that I designated as protological and eschatological, respectively. We can thus plot my original typology as a grid:

Table 1. Types of Christian Universalism

	God	human person
past	protological theoactualism	protological anthropoactualism
present/future	eschatological theoactualism	eschatological anthropoactualism

28. Parry and Partridge, introduction to *Universal Salvation?*, xvii.
29. David W. Congdon, *The God Who Saves: A Dogmatic Sketch* (Eugene, OR: Cascade Books, 2016), 3–12.

My excessively syllabic categories were a crude attempt to sup-
ply a more logical distinction between positions—as well as an
effort to see commonalities between otherwise opposed theologies. The typology was mostly a way of distinguishing my position
from the Protestant alternatives that were most on my mind at the
time—namely, Barthian universalism and evangelical universalism. The category of protological anthropoactualism was not a
viable option,[30] so the possible positions were these:

Table 2. Types of Protestant Universalism

	God	human person
past	Barthian universalism	n/a
present/future	existential universalism	evangelical universalism

As useful as this rubric might be, the obvious drawback with
this way of organizing the positions is the overly simplistic distinction between God and the human person, highlighted by the
absence of early Christian or patristic accounts of universalism.
To be sure, all three theologies in table 2 involve both God and the
human person, and the latter is both the object of God's saving
work and the subject of this work's completion. But the Protestant context of that typology requires a sharp distinction between
divine and human agency, given the forensic understanding of
salvation bequeathed to those in that tradition by the Reformers.
As a result, however much Protestants acknowledge the involve-
ment of both agents, salvation within this theological tradition is

30. In my framework, the human person anthropoactualism has in view is the
person here and now in the present, and obviously that person cannot have achieved
their salvation in the distant past before they existed, so protological anthropoactualism is a contradiction. One could argue that the person referred to here is the person
of Jesus Christ himself, but in that case the category of protological anthropoactualism would be identical to the category of protological theoactualism—Christ being
both divine and human.

understood fundamentally as a decision, an event, something that
has a punctiliar character: there is a before, and there is an after.
And this decisional, forensic soteriology means that, ultimately,
only a single agent, either divine or human, is responsible for
actualizing one's salvation.

As Morwenna Ludlow's chapter indicates, however, early
Christian accounts of universalism do not fit neatly within this
framework. Even though, at the cosmic level, God is the effective
agent, achieving the redemption of all things through acts like
descending into hell and paying the ransom for humankind, at
the individual level salvation involves a pedagogic purgation and
sanctification of the soul—and the former is incomplete without
the latter. Ludlow also points out that, for theologians like Origen
and Gregory of Nyssa, this purificatory process occurs slowly, over
long eons of time, thus dissolving the distinction between past and
present/future. Early Christian universalism shares with evangelical universalism an emphasis on the conscious response of the
human person to the holy love of God, but it shares with Barth's
theology a greater emphasis on the cosmic scope of redemption.

We could therefore construct a relatively more accurate typology if we replace "God" and "human person," respectively, with
"unconscious" and "conscious," and replace "past" and "present/
future," respectively, with "cosmic" and "individual." But no matter how accurate the typology, at the end of the day this exercise
only highlights the final inadequacy of such labels. For the purposes of this book, we have instead stuck to the most descriptive
and useful categories: patristic, evangelical, post-Barthian, and
existential.

The Plan of the Book

The purpose of this volume is to introduce readers to four different
ways of thinking about Christian universalism. These positions by
no means exhaust the available options, but they represent clearly

distinct approaches to the question that highlight the different presuppositions and logics available for theorizing a universalist soteriology. The purpose of these chapters is not to find common ground and shared points of emphasis; doing so would produce a highly repetitive and uninteresting volume. As examples of Christian universalism, there is substantial overlap regarding the need for salvation and the centrality of Jesus Christ for the achievement of salvation. The many available works of universalist apologetics offer syntheses along these lines, and there is no need to repeat that work here. The aim of each chapter in this volume is instead to foreground the distinctive features of each approach to universalism, to highlight the *variety* internal not only to Christian theology in general but to Christian universalism in particular.

The opening chapter, by Morwenna Ludlow, surveys the distinctive features of early Christian universalism, represented especially by Origen of Alexandria, Gregory of Nyssa, and Maximus the Confessor. Ludlow highlights what makes patristic theologies of universal salvation uniquely *patristic*. She looks especially at four features: an idiosyncratic interpretation of scripture that made heavy use of intertextual allusions, with an eye toward the eschatological aim of the text; the tradition of the "harrowing of hell," which was often drawn from texts outside of the canon as we know it today; the cosmic scope of redemption, which included the possible redemption of fallen angels; and the progressive purification and transformation of each person, beginning in this life and extending into the afterlife, often involving painful punishment as a necessary part of the divine pedagogy.

The following chapter, by Robin Parry, looks at what he calls evangelical universalism, which, despite its historical location in modern Protestantism—that is to say, in the Protestant movements shaped by European Pietism beginning in the early eighteenth century—shares many features in common with patristic universalism. Using David Bebbington's so-called quadrilateral, Parry argues for the genuinely evangelical character of evangelical universalism by demonstrating the way it conforms to the four marks of crucicentrism, biblicism, conversionism, and activism. Much like with Bebbington's original rubric, the two most distinctive features are biblicism and conversionism. In contrast to patristic universalism, evangelical universalism, following the example of the Reformers, is committed to developing its theology according to the boundaries of the biblical text and historically adheres to a more literal hermeneutic. Evangelical universalism also emphasizes the soteriological necessity of personal conversion through the confession of Christ's lordship. Whereas patristic universalism sees salvation as a long, even infinite, process of purification and sanctification, evangelical universalism sees salvation as occurring in the punctiliar moment of turning from rejection to acceptance of Christ.

The third chapter, by Tom Greggs, examines the category of Barthian universalism—or "post-Barthian" universalism, as he calls it, in light of Barth's explicit disavowal of universal salvation. The relationship between Barth's theology and universalism has been a staple feature of the academic study of his work since the middle of the twentieth century, and regardless of where one falls in that debate, the fact remains that the fundamental contours of his theology lend themselves to a universalist soteriology. Greggs examines those contours in detail. He focuses on the universal logic of Barth's doctrine of election, with its emphasis that all are included in the humanity of Christ, who alone is the one rejected in our place and elected on our behalf. Barth's "Christocentric particularism" places the decisive weight, where the question of salvation is concerned, on Jesus Christ's life, death, and resurrection, without thereby denying the indispensable role of the community of faith and the response of the believer. Greggs argues that a post-Barthian universalism will avoid trading in general metaphysical principles and will instead understand soteriology in terms of the concrete historical particularity of Jesus. It will be a theology of Christ's victory, not the triumph of an abstract concept of grace.

In the final chapter, I offer my own, existential take on universalism, which is a refinement of the position I articulated in my 2016 book, *The God Who Saves: A Dogmatic Sketch*. My position originated out of the twin convictions that (a) only a universalist soteriology provides a credible understanding of God and (b) theology must remain agnostic at best about the afterlife—indeed, anything we say theologically ought to remain meaningful in the absence of human immortality or general resurrection. Existential universalism offers a theological position that embraces both convictions, thereby (hopefully) offering a theology that might speak meaningfully to those alienated from traditional, institutional Christianity. Existential universal salvation is not a doctrine of who is redeemed at the end of history but rather a doctrine of where God is present in the midst of history. To develop this position, I draw on Dietrich Bonhoeffer's insight regarding "unconscious Christianity," and I connect this idea to an existential reconstruction of a Pauline theology of the cross filtered through the lens of liberation theology. I conclude with reflections on the purpose of any soteriology, existential or otherwise. In contrast to theologies that confidently proclaim all will be made right by God in the end, existential universalism instead offers a word of sustenance and stimulation for those who understand that the task of emancipation is not God's responsibility but ours.

The volume has no conclusion because there is no argument to conclude. These chapters do not exhaust the possibilities but rather invite readers to explore them—and to propose varieties of their own.[31] This book exists to welcome people into a lively

31. No book is ever truly comprehensive, and this book is no exception. Ideally, this book would include chapters on hopeful universalism (the position that universal salvation is something for which we can at best hope), pluralist universalism (the position that there are multiple ways to reach salvation or ultimate reality), and liberationist universalism (the position that salvation for all will be achieved when socioeconomic emancipation and equality is fully realized). The pluralist position should also go beyond Hick's approach to include David Ray Griffin's "deep pluralism" and the "relational pluralism" of John Thatamanil. See David Ray Griffin, *Deep*

conversation, one that invites disagreement and constructive ideas for the future. The goal of showcasing the diversity within the discourse about universal salvation is not to pit them against one another—as if only one, in the end, can be legitimate. Different theologies speak to different people in different contexts and at different times. This always has been and always will be the case. By placing these versions of universalism alongside one another, our hope is that they will bear witness both to the differences that are necessarily part of the human enterprise of God-talk and to the divine reality that lies beyond this enterprise, toward which we strive, even if for now we see this reality only indirectly, as "in a mirror" (1 Cor. 13:12).

Religious Pluralism (Louisville: Westminster John Knox, 2005); John J. Thatamanil, *Circling the Elephant: A Comparative Theology of Religious Diversity* (New York: Fordham University Press, 2020).

1

Patristic Universalism

Morwenna Ludlow

It is evident that many later expositions of universal salvation have either appealed to the fathers of the early church as authorities or at least mentioned them as evidence for a particular idea, or a particular reading of the Bible. In order to confront the obvious criticism that the idea that eventually all will be saved is at least unusual or unorthodox, if not outright heretical, many modern theologians have appealed implicitly or explicitly to the concept of a minority Christian tradition—an underground tradition, an idea that will not go away. The reasons for doing so are clear; the effect is to cast light on the similarities between various versions of the idea, rather than on their differences. While I would still wish to acknowledge the important continuities, my purpose in this chapter is to ask what aspects of early confessions of universal salvation were *distinctive* to the first millennium of Christianity.

Consequently, this chapter should be read with caution: it is *not* my attempt at an overarching summary of the most important, the most persuasive, or even the most prevalent features of early Christian universalism. It is highly selective; and, because I have been asked to focus on distinctive features, it is selective of those elements that might appear most culturally alien—and that might appear to present the least good arguments, even perhaps the least orthodox arguments, for universalism. Nevertheless, this survey reveals much of interest and of value to theological reflection, not least because of early Christians' constant dialogue with scripture and their concern to balance cosmic speculation with pastorally sensitive theology.

As I have already suggested, some of the features of early Christian universalism recur in later theology. A lot of discussion revolves around the nature of God, especially the divine attributes of justice and mercy (or love). This is particularly dominant in Origen's theology. Theodicy is a recurring theme (again, notably in Origen), although expressed in different ways from the modern debate. The ancients are typically more perplexed by the ultimate fates of the unjust who prosper and the just who suffer in this life (hence the recurring motif of Dives and Lazarus) than by the fates of those who have not heard the gospel or those of other faiths— two themes that have propelled much modern discussions of universalism. However, as we shall see, early Christians did ponder the destiny of those who died before the advent of Jesus Christ and of good pagans (see below, "'The Harrowing of Hell'—the Canon and Beyond"). Although some modern scholars have criticized ancient universalism for a lack of explicit christological content, it is, like most present-day Christian universalism, in fact fundamentally predicated on what God has done for his world through the incarnation, death, and resurrection of his Son Jesus Christ.

Like modern theologians, early Christians grappled with the Bible's witness to salvation, noting the difficulties of drawing a simple picture from the various declarations, stories, and warnings about the possibility of salvation. But the way they engage with the Bible is inevitably colored by their intellectual and cultural context. Although they have sometimes been accused of "proof-texting," because of their habit of directly quoting only one verse here and one verse there, a closer investigation of their exegetical practice reveals that they, in fact, often have a longer portion of biblical text in mind, while they quote only a fraction of it word for word. Naturally, early theologians do not read the Bible from a modern historical-critical perspective, but they often employ the intellectual tools of their own day to the text—using grammar, etymology, and the rhetorical analysis of argument, for example, to elucidate a difficult text. They frequently step back from offering a definitive exegesis of a particular text, sometimes offering two or more tentative interpretations. A further factor to take into consideration is that, until the mid-fourth century, the canon of the New Testament was not settled. As a result, early Christian advocates of the doctrine of universal salvation regularly appeal to texts that are not in the modern canon (at least not in its Western variants; see again below, "'The Harrowing of Hell'—the Canon and Beyond"). Some of these texts are seemingly appealed to not so much for scriptural authority as for evidence of common or traditional practices, such as prayers for the dead. The first section of this chapter will therefore deal with the distinctive ways in which early Christians advocated universalism by appealing to tradition. Because of the reasons stated above, "tradition" is understood broadly as comprising (what we would now recognize as) the biblical canon, other early Christian texts, and Christian practice (including sacraments and prayers).

Much modern debate has tended to focus on the fates of contemporary humans: What will happen to my good Muslim neighbor? What will happen to those in parts of the world where the gospel has not been heard? What about those humans who are seemingly unable from physical or mental impairment to respond to God's call? Although early Christian theologians were clearly

concerned for the fates of their neighbors, their universalism typically had a thoroughly cosmic dimension, opening out beyond
a concern for contemporary humans to the whole human race
(past and future); to all rational creation (including angels and—
sometimes—fallen angels); and, in some cases, to a hope for the
renewal of the whole creation. This cosmic hope was the form in
which early universal salvation was typically expressed and will
be the subject of the second section of this chapter.

Although this cosmic dimension might seem to erode the contours of the historical and the particular, this was not in fact the
case. Of course, modern theology has had to grapple with the
tension between a belief in God's particular care and a hope for
the expansiveness of his salvation.[1] But in the third section of this
chapter, I will suggest the distinctive ways in which early Christians
held this tension and, in particular, the ways in which it affected
their concept of the spiritual (and the ascetic) life.

Tradition

Universalism as a Tradition in Eastern Christian Theology

One thing that becomes very clear from familiarity with early
Greek Christian theology is that those who expressed a belief in
the salvation of all were either working from within a particular
tradition or at least engaging closely with it. There is little evidence
that individual theologians were coming up with this idea independently. This is not to say, however, that all versions of the doctrine
were the same, or that they can all be referred to as "Origenist"—
although Origen clearly was the dominant influence. Origen himself was influenced by prior thinkers in Alexandria, especially
Clement. And those who followed him engaged critically with
his ideas. For example, while accepting the fundamental basis of

---

1. This has been shown superbly by Tom Greggs. See Tom Greggs, *Barth, Origen,
and Universal Salvation: Restoring Particularity* (Oxford: Oxford University Press, 2009).

Origen's hope for the salvation of all, Gregory of Nyssa critiqued
Origen's doctrine of the resurrection of the body and significantly
nuanced the concept of the afterlife with his distinctive concept of
epektasis, or perpetual progress.[2] The reception of Origen's ideas
further east, in the Syriac-speaking parts of the Roman Empire
and beyond, had its own distinctive flavor too, being combined
with ideas that were less commonly found in the Greek and Latin
speaking worlds (such as "soul sleep") and being expressed in the
context of local liturgical and ascetic practice.[3]

However, exact lines of evidence are difficult to trace. Ancient
writers were, of course, centuries away from modern apparatuses
such as footnotes and bibliographies, and they often omitted the
names of those with whose ideas they were engaging in constructive critique. (Far more often, they named and quoted those with
whom they radically disagreed, as in Origen's *Against Celsus*.)
Frequently, we can only guess at what books a certain author had
read. The matter is made more complex still by evidence that some
texts expressing universalism may have been edited in their later
reception, further confusing the ways in which they themselves
were receiving earlier universalist ideas. The essential point to note,
then, is that it was far from the case that thinkers simply either were
or were not universalist: there were a variety of arguments and a
plethora of different expressions of the view in different contexts.

Scripture

The one passage above all that dominates early Christian discussion of universal salvation is 1 Corinthians 15:28: "When all things
are subjected to him, then the Son himself will also be subjected
to the one who put all things in subjection under him, so that God
may be all in all." Early universalists often refer in brief to God's

2. Morwenna Ludlow, *Universal Salvation: Eschatology in the Thought of Gregory
of Nyssa and Karl Rahner* (Oxford: Clarendon, 2000), 49, 63–64, 68–73.

3. Brian E. Daley, *The Hope of the Early Church* (Peabody, MA: Hendrickson,
2003), 175–78.

promise that God will be "all in all." This text's authoritative
weight was due to the fact that it came from Paul, "the Apostle,"
and from a letter that was absolutely central to the identity of
early Christians. First Corinthians 15:28 was often read in parallel with other Pauline texts, especially Ephesians 3:18–19 ("I pray
that you may have the power to comprehend, with all the saints,
what is the breadth and length and height and depth, and to know
the love of Christ that surpasses knowledge, so that you may be
filled with all the fullness of God") and the christological hymn
in Philippians 2:7–11:

> And being found in human form,
>   he humbled himself
>   and became obedient to the point of death—
>   even death on a cross.
>
> Therefore God also highly exalted him
>   and gave him the name
>   that is above every name,
> so that at the name of Jesus
>   every knee should bend,
>   in heaven and on earth and under the earth,
> and every tongue should confess
>   that Jesus Christ is Lord,
>   to the glory of God the Father.

While it would not be fair to say early Christians were unique
in using such verses to ground their belief in universal salvation, it
is fair to claim that *the way* they interpreted them bore the typical
character of early Christian biblical exegesis. In particular, the use
of a set of passages that were understood to mutually interpret one
another is a very distinctive aspect of early Christian universalist
readings of the Bible.[4] Together, these three texts, understood in

4. Steve Harmon, "The Subjection of All Things in Christ: The Christocentric Universalism of Gregory of Nyssa (331/340–ca. 395)," in *"All Shall Be Well": Explorations*

the contexts of their respective epistles, witnessed not only to the hope for universal salvation but also to its grounding in the incarnation (Phil. 2), the cross (Phil. 2; Eph. 3, with the "breadth and length and height and depth" often taken to indicate the cross),[5] and the resurrection (1 Cor. 15). But we can say something more specific still; in order to do so, we will consider three distinctive features that I take to be typical of early Christian exegetical practice as these exegetes engaged with texts that were considered to teach universalism: intertextuality, following the order and aim, and literary training.

Intertextuality

At the end of Origen's great work *On First Principles*, he discusses "the end and consummation of all things."[6] This phrase in itself appears to allude to a phrase in Acts 3:21. Origen does not obviously take more from that text, although it may bolster his conviction that the consummation will be brought about through Christ.[7] *On First Principles* 3.6 is, in effect, a commentary or reflection on 1 Corinthians 15, which Origen mentions or alludes

---

in *Universalism and Christian Theology, from Origen to Moltmann*, ed. Gregory MacDonald (Eugene, OR: Cascade Books, 2011), esp. 49–50.

5. See, e.g., Gregory of Nyssa, *On the Three-Day Period of the Resurrection of Our Lord Jesus Christ*, in *The Easter Sermons of Gregory of Nyssa: Translation and Commentary: Proceedings of the Fourth International Colloquium on Gregory of Nyssa, Cambridge, England: 11–15 September, 1978*, ed. Andreas Spira and Christoph Klock, trans. Stuart G. Hall, Patristics Monograph Series IX (Cambridge, MA: Philadelphia Patristics Foundation, 1981), 46–47. Hereafter this work is cited as *On the Three-Day Period*, trans. Hall. For the Greek text, see Gregory of Nyssa, "De Tridui Spatio," in *Sermones: Pars I*, ed. Ernestus Gebhardt, Gregorii Nysseni Opera IX (Leiden: Brill, 1992), 299.12–301.1. Hereafter this work is cited as GNO IX.

6. *De Principiis (On First Principles)* 3.6.1. Hereafter this work is cited as *DP*. Quotations of this source have been taken from the English translation Origen, *On First Principles: A Reader's Edition*, trans. John Behr (Oxford: Oxford University Press, 2019).

7. Acts 3:19–21: "Repent . . . so that your sins may be wiped out, so that times of refreshing may come from the presence of the Lord, and that he may send the Messiah appointed for you, that is, Jesus, who must remain in heaven until the time of universal restoration that God announced long ago through his holy prophets." Origen appears to allude to this text twice in *DP* 3.6.

to throughout. His interpretation centers on the promise of 1 Corinthians 15:28 (quoted repeatedly in 3.6.1–3 and again in 3.6.8),
which Origen interprets in the context of the rest of chapter 15 and
1 Corinthians as a whole.[8] Origen frequently quotes or alludes to
other Pauline texts, including the book of Hebrews (which Origen
regarded as Pauline in theology, if not in actual authorship).[9] He
has recourse to Johannine literature and Matthew's Gospel.[10] Genesis is a further important point of reference,[11] but Origen also
makes use of Exodus, Deuteronomy, Job, a psalm, Amos, Wisdom,
and the book of Revelation.[12] Origen's technique of reference is
so allusive it is likely there are more references that I have not
noted. Rather than working through 1 Corinthians 15 verse by
verse, Origen circles around it, repeatedly coming back to verse
28 and relating it to Paul's theology of the resurrection in chapter
15 as a whole. Particular points are reinforced either with explicit
reference to a text ("Moses, before all others, points to it"; "the
Apostle John more openly and clearly determines this to be the
case, when speaking thus"; "the Lord himself, in the Gospels, also
points out"[13]) or simply by inserting an allusion or quotation in
the flow of Origen's own prose. This technique is what Frances
Young has described as a patristic form of "intertextuality."[14]

Following the Order and Aim

While Origen's technique, especially in *On First Principles*, is
to weave a kind of fine tissue of allusions to scripture, Gregory

8. Origen quotes or alludes to 1 Cor. 15 at least half a dozen times (beyond references to 1 Cor. 15:28) and to other chapters of 1 Cor. at least three further times.

9. Rom. 8:21; 9:21; 2 Cor. 4:18; 5:1; Gal. 3:24; 4:2; Heb. 4:9; 8:5, 13; 9:15; 10:1; 12:24.

10. John 10:30; 17:21, 22, 24; 1 John 3:2; Matt. 5:4; 19:26.

11. Gen. 1:1, 26–28; 2:7, 17; 3:19; 18:27.

12. Exod. 25:40; Deut. 4:38; Job 42:2; Ps. 36:11; Amos 5:8; Wis. 1:14; Rev. 14:6.
(Numbering of OT texts follows the LXX.)

13. *DP* 3.6.1.

14. Frances Margaret Young, *Biblical Exegesis and the Formation of Christian
Culture* (Cambridge: Cambridge University Press, 1997), 97–99, 108–9.

of Nyssa is typically more concerned with what he perceived to be the order (*taxis*) and aim (*skopos*) of a text, or even of a whole biblical book.[15] This is perhaps most obvious in *The Life of Moses*, where Gregory first summarizes the biblical account in his own words and then offers a theological reflection on it, based on the assumption that Moses's own life maps onto the progress of a human soul. Thus the final biblical words about Moses, describing his failure to reach the promised land yet nevertheless affirming that he was loved by God, seem to be taken by Gregory to indicate the idea of the soul's perpetual progress toward the divine (of which, more below). It is less obvious to modern readers that other parts of the Bible have a similar order. Yet Gregory discerns it, for example, in the Beatitudes from the Sermon on the Mount (Matt. 5:1–11) and in the collection of the Psalms. In each of these cases, he argues that the sequence represents the progress of human souls. For example, Gregory follows tradition in believing the Psalter to be divided into five sections; his originality is in the claim that in each section "the Word has observed some particular good through which blessedness comes about for us from God in accordance with some sequential order of the good things beheld in each section, always carrying the soul on to what is more sublime until it reaches the peak of good things."[16] This "peak of good things" is revealed in Psalm 150. Consequently, he reads this psalm eschatologically, seeing in the harmony of the musicians the eschatological universal salvation of the whole cosmos:

> In this psalm, all things which exist will be holy after the complete destruction of evil, and all things will praise God in harmony when they have equally acquired immutability in respect to evil *in the*

15. For this contrast and a more detailed exposition of the points I make in summary here, see Morwenna Ludlow, "Theology and Allegory: Origen and Gregory of Nyssa on the Unity and Diversity of Scripture," *International Journal of Systematic Theology* 4, no. 1 (2002): 45–66, esp. 50, 52, 53–55.

16. Gregory of Nyssa, *Treatise on the Inscriptions of the Psalms*, trans. Ronald E. Heine (Oxford: Oxford University Press, 1995), 1.114. See also 1.120.

firmness of his *power* (Ps. 150:1), and have lifted up together the sound of praise to *his greatness* (v. 2) as if with the loud blast of a *trumpet* (v. 3). Whenever the whole creation, consisting of all things superior and all things inferior has been united in one choir, both the spiritual creation and that which has been separated and has been at a distance on account of sin will produce the good sound, like a *cymbal* (v. 5) from our concord.[17]

Literary Training

As has been well documented in recent research, early Christian exegesis was profoundly affected by the way in which leading thinkers had been educated.[18] Well into the Christian era, young men (Christian and non-Christian alike) continued to be educated through the reading and reciting of classical Greek (or in the West, Latin) literature; there were no specifically Christian schools,[19] and many of the great preachers had trained in schools of secular oratory. Modern patristic scholarship typically no longer sees this as the corruption of Christian content by meretricious pagan forms (a literary parallel to the supposed corruption of Christianity by Hellenistic philosophy—also now largely rejected). Rather, scholars seek to show *how* Christians used rhetoric in biblical exegesis.

My example here is Gregory of Nyssa's *Treatise on 1 Corinthians 15:28*.[20] This is not an obviously rhetorical text. The modern edition gathers it together with other short dogmatic works, as if it belonged to a modern collection of essays on systematic

17. Gregory of Nyssa, *Inscriptions of the Psalms*, 1.121–22.

18. See esp. Averil Cameron, *Christianity and the Rhetoric of Empire: The Development of Christian Discourse* (Berkeley: University of California Press, 1994); Young, *Biblical Exegesis and the Formation of Christian Culture*; Margaret Mary Mitchell, *The Heavenly Trumpet: John Chrysostom and the Art of Pauline Interpretation* (Louisville: Westminster John Knox, 2002).

19. Until the "fall" of Rome, after which monasteries gradually took over many of the educational roles formerly played by secular teachers. See Roger Rees, "Education and Schools, Latin," in *The Oxford Dictionary of Late Antiquity* (Oxford: Oxford University Press, 2018).

20. Often known by the Latin title: *In illud: tunc et ipse filius*.

theology. However, it is probably better understood as a kind of commentary on one verse in the context of 1 Corinthians 15, but one best understood as thoroughly shaped by the discipline of rhetoric, which taught students not only to construct their own texts but thoroughly to analyze others' texts.[21] Unlike Origen's free-wheeling approach to 1 Corinthians 15, discussed above, Gregory's approach is much more systematic, much more careful. One might also say, however, that it is much more contrived and even disingenuous—for while highlighting the idea that the mention of the "submission" of the Son in 1 Corinthians 15:28 does not entail an unorthodox doctrine of the Trinity, Gregory slips in his universalistic understanding of the same verse. In the course of his argument, he uses intertextual reference to other parts of scripture (especially the Psalms and John's Gospel).[22] But he also uses grammatical analysis, asking questions such as, What are the possible meanings of *hypotassō* (submit) in the Bible, and which one is in play here?[23] He contextualizes 1 Corinthians 15:28 by asking, What is Paul's *argument* (*logos*) in the whole of chapter 15?[24] He sets out the meaning of 1 Corinthians 15:22–28 in his own words (this yields one of Gregory's clearest assertions of universal salvation), then supports his interpretation by further reference to Paul.[25] This latter strategy involves Gregory in a theological

21. For a detailed argument to this effect, see Morwenna Ludlow, "III.2 In Illud: Tunc et Ipse Filius," in *Gregory of Nyssa: The Minor Treatises on Trinitarian Theology and Apollinarism: Proceedings of the 11th International Colloquium on Gregory of Nyssa, Tübingen, 17–20 September 2008*, ed. Volker Henning Drecoll and Margitta Berghaus (Leiden: Brill, 2011).

22. Gregory of Nyssa, *In illud: tunc et ipse filius*, in *Gregorii Nysseni opera dogmatica minora, Pars II*, ed. J. Kenneth Downing, Jacobus A. McDonough, and Hadwig Hörner, Gregorii Nysseni Opera III/2 (Leiden: Brill, 1987), 4.15–5.8; 21.17–19. For a translation (indicating page numbers of the Greek text) see Gregory of Nyssa, "On 'Then Also the Son Himself Will Be Subjected to the One Who Subjected All Things to Him,'" in *One Path for All: Gregory of Nyssa on the Christian Life and Human Destiny*, trans. Rowan A. Greer and J. Warren Smith, 118–32 (Eugene, OR: Cascade Books, 2015).

23. Gregory of Nyssa, *In illud: tunc et ipse filius* 5.12–6.10.

24. Gregory of Nyssa, *In illud: tunc et ipse filius* 10.5.

25. Gregory of Nyssa, *In illud: tunc et ipse filius* 13.17–20; 13.22–14.7.

explication of what Paul meant by the "body of Christ"—for it
is that which is submitted to the Father at the end.[26] Finally, he
defends Paul's use of words in their less-than-usual sense.[27]

"The Harrowing of Hell"—the Canon and Beyond

The "harrowing of hell" is a later term used to describe Christ's
descent to preach to the dead (and, in some versions, to offer or
give them salvation). Matthew 12:40 and the Apostles' Creed's
statement that Christ rose "from the dead" (*a mortuis*) are just two
pieces of evidence for the common belief among early Christians
that, for a period after the crucifixion, Jesus Christ was not merely
dead but dwelt with those who were dead (the descent or *descensus*
motif).[28] The concept of the harrowing of hell turned this sojourn
from Jesus's passive experience of death into the active continuation of his work of revelation and salvation. It was sometimes
used to explain how the just people of God from the times before
the incarnation (especially the patriarchs and prophets) were able
to be saved. More broadly, it was used to explain the salvation of
(or offer of salvation to) further categories of people: the just in
general, or sometimes all people.[29] This doctrine is by no means
articulated by all those early Christians who teach universal salvation, nor does it necessarily entail universal salvation (for it was
articulated in various forms). However, it is a narrative or mythical answer to a crucial question: *If* God will save all people, what
about those who died before being baptized or repenting? What
about those who died before the coming of Christ? Thus, although
it is not a ubiquitous feature of early universalism, it is to my mind

26. Gregory of Nyssa, *In illud: tunc et ipse filius* 18.16–25.
27. Gregory of Nyssa, *In illud: tunc et ipse filius* 25.10–28.
28. Matt. 12:40: "For just as Jonah was three days and three nights in the belly
of the sea monster, so for three days and three nights the Son of Man will be in the
heart of the earth."
29. For a review of this motif, see Jeffrey A. Trumbower, *Rescue for the Dead: The
Posthumous Salvation of Non-Christians in Early Christianity* (New York: Oxford
University Press, 2001), esp. chap. 5.

a distinctive element. Those rare modern theologians who use it in their own teaching have clearly been influenced by the fathers (see, e.g., Hans Urs von Balthasar's teaching on Holy Saturday[30]).

First Peter 3:18–20 and 4:6 were taken by some early Christians to mean that Christ preached to the dead in order that his salvation might be offered genuinely to all (although modern scholars would insist that these verses are capable of various interpretations):

> For Christ also suffered for sins once for all, the righteous for the unrighteous, in order to bring you to God. He was put to death in the flesh, but made alive in the spirit, in which also he went and made a proclamation to the spirits in prison, who in former times did not obey, when God waited patiently in the days of Noah, during the building of the ark, in which a few, that is, eight persons, were saved through water. . . .
>
> For this is the reason the gospel was proclaimed even to the dead, so that, though they had been judged in the flesh as everyone is judged, they might live in the spirit as God does.

The verses from chapters 3 and 4 were read together to imply that Christ not only preached to but saved the disobedient spirits.[31] Thus, this expanded on a tradition that Christ descended to rescue the righteous men and women of the Old Testament.[32] The preaching to the dead theme was recapitulated in other apocryphal Petrine texts (the second-century Gospel of Peter and Apocalypse of Peter).[33] It seems likely that these narrative texts that indicate

30. Hans Urs von Balthasar, *Dare We Hope "That All Men Be Saved"? With a Short Discourse on Hell* (San Francisco: Ignatius Press, 1988); Hans Urs von Balthasar, *Mysterium Paschale: The Mystery of Easter*, trans. Aidan Nichols (Edinburgh: T&T Clark, 1990), chap. 4.

31. Trumbower, *Rescue for the Dead*, 96; Ilaria Ramelli, *The Christian Doctrine of Apokatastasis: A Critical Assessment from the New Testament to Eriugena*, Supplements to Vigiliae Christianae 120 (Leiden: Brill, 2013), 42.

32. Trumbower, *Rescue for the Dead*, 92–94.

33. On the Gospel of Peter: Trumbower, 96; Ramelli, *Apokatastasis*, 42–43. On the Apocalypse of Peter: Ramelli, *Apokatastasis*, 67–71.

the possibility of postmortem salvation (rather than universal salvation as such) were read in the light of another Petrine source,
2 Peter 3:9: "The Lord is not slow about his promise, as some think
of slowness, but is patient with you, not wanting any to perish,
but all to come to repentance."

The early second-century Shepherd of Hermas (a visionary text
included in some early canons of the New Testament) is cautious,
suggesting that not Christ but forty of his apostles preached to
and baptized the dead and that only the righteous will be rescued
in this way.[34] Other early texts are bolder, expressing the idea that
Christ went to *convert* those of the dead who had rejected God.
For example, the early second-century Syriac text Odes of Solomon imagines Christ speaking of his descent:

> I did not perish although they thought it of me. Sheol saw me and
> was shattered, and Death ejected me and many with me. . . . I went
> down with it as far as its depth. . . . And I made a congregation of
> the living among his dead; and I spoke with them by living lips;
> in order that my word may not fail. And those who had died ran
> toward me; and they cried out and said, "Son of God, have pity
> on us . . . ." Then I heard their voice, and placed their faith upon
> my heart. And I placed my name upon their head, because they
> are free and they are mine.[35]

Such texts are evidence of a deeply rooted belief that Christ's
descent to the dead had a purpose. The tradition was well-known
enough to be a bone of contention for the second-century pagan
Celsus.[36] The harrowing-of-hell texts were read alongside a longstanding Christian hope that the prayers of the living might be able
to change the circumstances of the dead. Such a hope is evident,

34. Trumbower, *Rescue for the Dead*, 47–49.
35. "Odes of Solomon," in *The Old Testament Pseudepigrapha*, trans. James
H. Charlesworth (Garden City, NY: Doubleday, 1983), 771 (Odes 42.10–12, 14–15,
19–20). For further analysis, see Trumbower, *Rescue for the Dead*, 96.
36. Origen, *Contra Celsum* 2.43, quoted in Trumbower, *Rescue for the Dead*, 100.

for example, in the Acts of Paul and Thecla and the Passion of Perpetua and Felicity (the former probably, and the latter certainly, second century).[37]

These traditions might seem somewhat esoteric to modern readers, but they had a clear influence on the doctrine of universal salvation. Clement of Alexandria's eschatology was shaped not only by his belief in purificatory punishment (for which, see below) but by texts such as 1 Peter, the Shepherd of Hermas, and probably the pseudepigraphical Petrine material.[38] Clement was a very thoughtful Christian theologian who, it seems, at the very least hoped for the salvation for all.[39] This tradition of Christ's salvific action after death not only gave Clement a reason for hope; it also offered him an answer to a perplexing question: If God wills all to be saved (1 Tim. 2:4), *how* might that be possible?

When challenged by Celsus's views, Origen defended the concept of Christ's salvific descent to the dead.[40] Origen is clear that Christ descended to Hades, the "holding place" for the souls of the dead, not Gehenna, the place of fiery punishment. In Hades Christ preached to "those of them who were willing to accept him, or those who, for reasons which he himself knew, he saw to be ready to do so." This slightly elliptical phrase suggests that, for Origen, the harrowing of hell brought salvation to some through Christ's preaching, but that others remained unconverted. Thus,

37. See Trumbower, *Rescue for the Dead*, 60–70, 80–89. See also, on the latter text, Brian E. Daley, *The Hope of the Early Church* (Peabody, MA: Hendrickson, 2003), 37.

38. Clement sometimes appears to equivocate over whether in Hades salvation was offered to all or merely to the just, but as Trumbower puts it, "his very equivocation indicates that the issue was a live one for him." Trumbower, *Rescue for the Dead*, 99–100, citing Clement, *Stromateis* 6.6.46. For Clement's use of the Shepherd of Hermas and the Petrine tradition, see also Ramelli, *Apokatastasis*, 43, 71, 126–27.

39. Daley notes that Clement expresses his hope "with great caution" (*Hope of the Early Church*, 47). Ramelli asserts that, for Clement, universal salvation is "hoped-for" (*Apokatastasis*, 119). Trumbower is less certain about Clement's stance (*Rescue for the Dead*, 99–100, 109–110).

40. Ramelli, *Apokatastasis*, 43, citing Origen, *Contra Celsum* 2.43 and *Homily on Samuel* 2.5.

God also used other means to secure the salvation of all.[41] Gregory of Nyssa's sermon *On the Three-Day Period of the Resurrection of Our Lord* reflects on the significance of the fact that Christ died in order to destroy death.[42] He combines the salvific descent of Christ with his famous "ransom" theory of the atonement: The "heart of the earth" is where death/Satan dwells, and death hopes it will conquer Christ through the crucifixion ("With this hope [death] receives in himself the one who through kindness visited those below").[43] But death's hopes are destroyed, for death is swallowed up (2 Cor. 5:4), the last enemy destroyed (1 Cor. 15:26)—and not by a mighty display of power but by "a simple and incomprehensible visit, a mere coming of Life and Light achieves for those sitting in darkness and death's shadow the utter eclipse and abolition of darkness and of death."[44]

The *descensus* motif occurs also in several other well-known early Christian thinkers—for example, Gregory of Nazianzus, Cyril of Alexandria, Hilary, Ambrosiaster, and Ambrose. All of these were inclined toward generous interpretations of Christ's salvation of the dead in Hades, although of these only Gregory had a clear hope for universal salvation.[45]

Cosmic Hope

Some (although by no means all) modern expressions of universal salvation seem to be somewhat anthropocentric. This may be because they are driven at least partly by theodicy or because it is difficult to envisage what salvation for the nonhuman creation might

41. Origen, *Contra Celsum* 2.43, trans. Henry Chadwick (Cambridge: Cambridge University Press, 1953). On Origen's distinction between Hades and Gehenna, see Trumbower, *Rescue for the Dead*, 100–101.

42. Gregory of Nyssa, GNO IX; Gregory of Nyssa, *On the Three-Day Period*, trans. Hall.

43. *On the Three-Day Period*, trans. Hall, 35–36; GNO IX, 281.2–16.

44. *On the Three-Day Period*, trans. Hall, 37; GNO IX, 285.3–6.

45. Trumbower, *Rescue for the Dead*, 102–3; Ramelli, *Apokatastasis*, 43.

mean. By contrast, many patristic expressions of universalism expand well beyond human beings—although their vision could still be called anthropocentric in that human nature, through the incarnation, is the means through which the whole universe is redeemed. (As we shall see below, this is a particularly dominant theme in Maximus.) However, this cosmic vision is expressed in different ways by different thinkers. Here I will briefly discuss Origen, Gregory of Nyssa, and Maximus the Confessor.

Origen

Origen's eschatology, especially as expressed in his work *On First Principles*, is notable for its cosmic scope. Origen writes about the fate of all creation and about the stretch of time from creation to consummation.[46] This expansiveness reflects not only the scriptural texts with which he engages but the alternative theologies, from Valentinians and others, that he was opposing and that had a similarly expansive scope.

Besides the repetition of Paul's promise that God will be "all in all" (1 Cor. 15:28), the other cosmic framing concept of Origen's eschatology is the idea that "the end is always like the beginning": "Therefore, as there is one end of all things, so ought there to be understood one beginning of all things, and as there is one end of many things, so also from one beginning there are many differences and varieties, which, in turn, through the goodness of God and by subjection to Christ and through the unity of the Holy Spirit, are recalled to one end which is like the beginning."[47]

The variety is caused, at least partly, by the freedom God gave creation—in particular, by the freedom of rational creatures to accept or reject him. By "one beginning" Origen means the beginning all creation had in the will of God: he firmly asserts the

46. See, e.g., *DP* 1.6.2; 3.6.2–3.
47. *DP* 1.6.2.

doctrine of creation out of nothing, so although he may assert
the preexistence of souls before their material bodies (his precise
views on this doctrine are disputed), he emphatically does not
think such souls were coeternal with God.[48] It is because of Origen's insistence that the end is like the beginning that it is fair to
categorize his eschatology as based on the idea of *apokatastasis*,
which in Greek means "restoration back to a previous state."
This is probably the single most distinctive aspect of Origen's
eschatology, viewed from a modern perspective.

But Origen's hope was not simply for an *apokatastasis*; it was
for an *apokatastasis tōn pantōn*—a restoration of *all* things.[49]
In this restoration, all will be subjected to God; evil will be destroyed, and consequently God will be "all in all."[50] The most
controversial aspect of this universal hope (and it is a *hope*,
expressed with caution[51]) is whether it includes the salvation of
the devil and other fallen angels (i.e., demons). So what does
Origen say about this? In *On First Principles*, at least, he cau-
tiously suggests that spiritual beings who have opposed God
will be transformed eventually by God's saving power. But the
emphasis on transformation is absolutely key. Origen writes that
the destruction of death, the last enemy, consists not in the annihilation of its "substance which was made by God," but of
its "hostile purpose and will": "It is destroyed, therefore, not in
the sense that it shall not be, but that it shall not be an enemy
and death."[52] If the devil is saved, then, one might say that he is

---

48. Greggs, *Barth, Origen, and Universal Salvation*, chap. 3; Tom Greggs, "Apokatastasis: Particularist Universalism in Origen (c. 185–c. 254)," in MacDonald, "*All
Shall Be Well*," 32. Mark Julian Edwards challenges the conventional reading of Origen on this question (*Origen against Plato* [Aldershot, UK: Ashgate, 2002], 93–97)
as does John Behr (introduction to *On First Principles*, by Origen [Oxford: Oxford
University Press, 2019], lxxix–lxxxviii). Both Edwards and Behr draw attention to
the poor textual editions that led to earlier readings.

49. As stated above, the phrase comes from Acts 3:21, the theology from 1 Cor. 15.

50. *DP* 1.6.2; 3.3.1–3; 3.6.5.

51. See, e.g., *DP* 1.6.1.

52. *DP* 3.6.5.

destroyed as the devil—that is, he is destroyed as a fallen angel but saved as an angel.

A second aspect of the salvation of all things is the restoration of the material creation. Although Origen opposes those whose Christian hope is overly invested in the expectation of material reward,[53] he does not himself abandon a hope for materiality. He denies, for example, that the material creation will be annihilated: "For if the heavens are to be changed, assuredly that which is changed does not perish; and if the form of the world passes away, it is not, by any means, an annihilation or destruction of the material substance that is indicated, but a kind of change of quality and transformation of form takes place."[54]

Thus Origen defends the resurrection of the body, albeit in a refined and spiritual form, paying close attention to Paul's concept of the spiritual body and his grain of wheat metaphor in 1 Corinthians 15.[55] The most distinctive feature of Origen's eschatological hope for materiality, therefore, is a hope for its transformation, "gradually and by degrees, during the passing of infinite and immeasurable ages."[56] Previously, Origen research had tended to focus on the restoration of *rational* creation. However, although the precise nature of the resurrection body for Origen remains somewhat obscure, more recent research has stressed the importance of materiality in his cosmology, not least through his doctrine of the Son. For while he fully affirmed the reality of the incarnation (most famously against Celsus), Origen also had a doctrine of what we might call the "cosmic Christ"—Christ pervading all creation. This is expressed by Origen in his doctrine of Christ's *epinoiai* or "titles," which express what Christ is both in himself and *for creation*: "In [Christ's] being Wisdom, there is in him the blueprint for *all* the world. . . . The *epinoiai* are, therefore,

53. *DP* 2.11.2.
54. *DP* 1.6.4.
55. *DP* 2.10.3.
56. *DP* 3.6.6.

the way in which the One God reaches out to the plurality and diversity of *all* creation."[57]

Gregory of Nyssa

The cosmic scope of Gregory's hope is most boldly expressed in what he takes to be the implication of Paul's proclamation that God will be "all in all": the complete elimination of evil.[58] In some places this idea is traced out with philosophical analysis. Gregory believes that evil is, strictly speaking, nonbeing; it was not created by God, and it is thus an impermanent feature of the cosmos. That is not to say that evil is not dangerous, nor that it could have been eliminated in any way other than through Christ. But it is to say that once evil has been separated from the good in which it subsists, evil will cease to exist.[59] In other places, Gregory focuses on the consequences of this for his audience. For example, his sermon *On the Three-Day Period of the Resurrection of Our Lord* spells them out in more detail:

> Do you want to know the enormous number of those restored in so short a time? Count for me all the intervening generations of men from the first inroad of evils until their abolition, how many people in every generation, reckoned in how many millions! Is it possible for the number to be quantified, when evil spread out with their successions and the evil wealth of wickedness being

57. Greggs, "Apokatastasis," 38, quoting Jean Daniélou, *Origen*, trans. Walter Mitchell (London: Sheed and Ward, 1955), 257. See also Rowan D. Williams, "The Son's Knowledge of the Father in Origen," in *Origeniana Quarta: Die Referate des 4. Internationalen Origenskongresses (Innsbruck, 2.–6. September 1985)*, ed. Lothar Lies (Innsbruck: Tyrolia-Verlag, 1987), 147; Rowan D. Williams, "Origen: Between Orthodoxy and Heresy," in *Origeniana Septima: Origenes in den Auseinandersetzungen des 4. Jahrhunderts*, ed. Wolfgang A Bienert and Uwe Kühneweg (Leuven: Leuven University Press, 1999), 12–13.

58. Gregory of Nyssa, *In illud: tunc et ipse filius* 13.23–14.1.

59. Ludlow, *Universal Salvation*, 86–89; Alden A. Mosshammer, "Evil," in *The Brill Dictionary of Gregory of Nyssa*, ed. Lucas F. Mateo Seco and Giulio Maspero (Leiden: Brill, 2010), 325–30.

divided between individuals became greater in every one? And so evil multiplied and went through every generation in succession, swelling in quantity ad infinitum, until it advanced to the climax of all evil and seized control of the whole of human nature.[60]

Gregory's consistent line is that Christ defeated *all* evil through the cross and resurrection. With the destruction of evil, humanity itself, however corrupt, will be released, not destroyed: "But instead of [humanity] sin will be destroyed and will be reduced to non-being."[61] A possible broader cosmic outcome of this view is that even evil in demons and the devil will be destroyed. Thus, in Gregory's dialogue *On the Soul and the Resurrection*, his sister Macrina reports that "some say" that those "under the earth" in Philippians 2:10 are demons or spirits opposed to that which is good. According to this view, "when evil shall have some day been annihilated in the long revolutions of the ages, nothing shall be left outside the world of goodness, but that even from those evil spirits shall rise in harmony the confessions of Christ's Lordship."[62]

Gregory's caution in presenting the cosmic scope of salvation as a *possibility* can be explained by the controversy over Origen's idea that the devil would be saved. But the fact that he mentions it at all might also be explained by his desire to avoid a further controversial aspect of Origenistic eschatology. Many believed (quite possibly erroneously) that Origen's theology implied future falls would be possible even after humanity is saved. Gregory's approach suggests that he thinks that one way of preventing further falls is the elimination of evil in demons, those beings who lure humans away from the good.

60. *On the Three-Day Period*, trans. Hall, 36–37; GNO IX, 283.11–224.
61. Gregory of Nyssa, *Inscriptions of the Psalms*, 2.283 (trans. adapted). For further confirmation that sinners will be not destroyed but reconciled, see Gregory of Nyssa, *In illud: tunc et ipse filius* 26.1–27.5, referring to Rom. 5:10.
62. Gregory of Nyssa, *On the Soul and the Resurrection*, trans. William Moore, *Nicene and Post-Nicene Fathers*, series 2, vol. 5 (Edinburgh: T&T Clark, 1994), 444.

If evil demons (i.e., fallen angels) might possibly be redeemed, Gregory is certain that humans will be restored to a harmony with the angels. Above, we quoted his interpretation of Psalm 150 as a hymn of cosmic harmony between human and angelic creation. Indeed, in that passage Gregory writes that "every breathing creature" will praise God.[63] Does that include animals? Gregory does not, to my knowledge, comment specifically on that point. When he comments on the beauty of "what is above the world," he does so only in very general terms, praising its "immaterial beauties, the thrones, rulers, powers, dominions (Col. 1:16), the hosts of angels, the church of the holy ones, the city on high, and the festival gathering above heaven of those enrolled."[64]

Maximus the Confessor

As Paul Blowers remarks, "Maximus has been called a *cosmic* theologian and rightly so. For Maximus the Confessor, the world—the natural world and the 'world' of the scriptural revelation—is the broad and complex theater in which God's incarnational mission is playing itself out to full completion."[65]

Extrapolating what this expansive, cosmic perspective on the "world" (*cosmos*, in Greek) means for Maximus's eschatology, however, is a complex task. To begin with, although there has been some scholarly debate on the matter (heightened by Hans Urs von Balthasar's influential use of Maximus's theology), most contemporary scholarship concurs that Maximus seems to be a hopeful,

63. Gregory of Nyssa, *Inscriptions of the Psalms*, 1.122–23.
64. Gregory of Nyssa, "In Regard to Those Fallen Asleep (*De Mortuis*)," in Greer and Smith, *One Path for All*, 100; GNO IX, 38.20–39.2.
65. Paul M. Blowers, introduction to *On the Cosmic Mystery of Jesus Christ: Selected Writings from St. Maximus the Confessor*, by St. Maximus the Confessor, trans. Robert Louis Wilken and Paul M. Blowers (Crestwood, NY: St. Vladimir's Seminary Press, 2003), 17, citing as evidence Lars Thunberg, *Man and the Cosmos: The Vision of St. Maximus the Confessor* (Crestwood, NY: St. Vladimir's Seminary Press, 1985); Lars Thunberg, *Microcosm and Mediator: The Theological Anthropology of Maximus the Confessor* (Chicago: Open Court, 1995).

rather than a certain, universalist—not least because he was writing in the period after Justinian's condemnations of a version of universalism.[66] There are frequent references in Maximus's works to the belief that only the "worthy" will be gathered up into a final salvation.[67] However, it would also be fair to say that Maximus's view was very expansive. Brian Daley writes, "For Maximus, the goal of history, as far as God's own plan is concerned, is clearly the salvation of the whole human race and the union of all creation with himself. . . . The heart of this eschatological renewal will be divinization, 'in which God is united with those who have become gods and makes everything his by his goodness.'"[68]

Like Origen and Gregory before him, Maximus links this hope to 1 Corinthians 15:28: "The one God, Creator of all is shown to reside proportionately in all beings through human nature. Things that are by nature separated from one another return to a unity as they converge together in the one human being. When this happens God will be *all in all* (1 Cor. 15:28), permeating all things and at the same time giving independent existence to all things in himself."[69] As this quotation suggests, the expansiveness of this vision depends on Maximus's theological anthropology and the fact that he saw humankind, perfected in Christ, as a cosmic mediator. God's creation not only "completed the primary principles (*logoi*) of creatures and the universal essences of creatures once and for all" but works providentially in all creatures for their "formation, progress, and sustenance."[70] Eschatologically, God is working toward a state in which "one and the same principle (*logos*) shall

66. Daley, *Hope of the Early Church*, 202, 263n96; Ramelli, *Apokatastasis*, 738.
67. See, e.g., Maximus, *Ambiguum 7*, in Maximus, *On the Cosmic Mystery*, 56; Maximus, *Ad Thalassium 22*, in Maximus, *On the Cosmic Mystery*, 118.
68. Daley, *Hope of the Early Church*, 201, quoting Maximus, *Ambiguum 7* (see Maximus, *On the Cosmic Mystery*, 63–64).
69. Maximus, *Ambiguum 7*, in Maximus, *On the Cosmic Mystery*, 66.
70. Maximus, *Ad Thalassium 2*, in Maximus, *On the Cosmic Mystery*, 99. These providential principles are also sown by God in scripture. See Blowers, introduction to *On the Cosmic Mystery*, by Maximus, 17.

be observable throughout the universe."[71] This is the deification
of the universe, carried out by the trinitarian God: "The Father
approves this work, the Son properly carries it out, and the Holy
Spirit essentially completes both the Father's approval of it all and
the Son's execution of it, in order that God the Trinity might be
through all and in all (Eph. 4:6)."[72]

How does the Son carry out this process of deification? Famously, Maximus asserts that human nature is a microcosm of
the universe: through human nature the diverse elements of the
universe can be held together. The incarnation was to be the "perfection and fulfilment" of humanity's task of cosmic mediation.[73]
Maximus writes, "For this reason the human person was intro-
duced last among beings, as a kind of natural bond mediating between the universal poles through their proper parts, and leading
into unity in itself those things that are naturally set apart from
one another by a great interval."[74]

But because of sin, human nature is unable to carry out this uni-
fication. The incarnation is thus the only means by which human
nature can fulfill its task.[75] Christ became "the perfect human
being" and "thus he fulfils the great purpose of God the Father,
to recapitulate everything both in heaven and earth in himself
(Eph. 1:10), *in whom everything has been created* (Col. 1:16)."[76]
In Christ the five divisions manifest in creation are overcome:
those between male and female, paradise and the inhabited world,
heaven and earth, the intelligible and the sensible, and God and
creation.[77] "Thus he divinely recapitulates the universe in himself,

---

71. Maximus, *Ad Thalassium* 2, in Maximus, *On the Cosmic Mystery*, 100.
72. Maximus, *Ad Thalassium* 2, in Maximus, *On the Cosmic Mystery*, 100–101.
73. Thunberg, *Man and the Cosmos*, 74.
74. Maximus, *Ambiguum* 41, in Andrew Louth, *Maximus the Confessor* (London: Routledge, 1996), 157.
75. Thunberg, *Man and the Cosmos*, 74; Maximus, *Ambiguum* 41, in Louth, *Maximus the Confessor*, 158.
76. Maximus, *Ambiguum* 41, in Louth, *Maximus the Confessor*, 159.
77. Maximus, *Ambiguum* 41, in Louth, *Maximus the Confessor*, 159–60.

showing that the whole creation exists as one, like another human being, completed by the gathering together of its parts one with another in itself."[78]

Progressive Personal Transformation

As suggested by the previous section, much patristic universalism is driven by a belief in the possibility that God can work a progressive transformation of his whole creation. As recent scholarship has stressed, it is this that preserves the *particularity* of salvation alongside its cosmic scope. But this also means that early Christian universalism has more pastoral implications than one might imagine on first sight. I will briefly explore this issue by looking at Origen and Gregory of Nyssa.

Origen

We noted above Origen's emphasis that the transformation of the cosmos comes about gradually, by slow degrees across long ages of time. This conception applies not only to his doctrine of the resurrection of the body but also to his teaching on the destiny of the soul. Although in some places he might sound as though he has a retributive theory of justice ("God will render to each one what is deserved"[79]), such statements seem designed to emphasize that people will pay what they owe *and no more*—with the long-term aim of showing that punishment is not eternal. In *On First Principles*, Origen is clear that punishment is aimed at a good end: the restoration or transformation of those who are punished.[80] He explains the effectiveness of punishment in various ways and with various metaphors. First, it is medicinal—applied by God even if it is painful, just as a good doctor prescribes unpleasant

78. Maximus, *Ambiguum* 41, in Louth, *Maximus the Confessor*, 160.
79. *DP* 1.6.1.
80. *DP* 1.6.3.

drugs or painful surgery for a good end.[81] Second, he thinks that
punishment operates through the pain generated by one's own
conscience as one faces one's sins in the light of God's judgment.
Thus, Isaiah 50:11 ("Walk in the light of your fire, and in the flame
which you have kindled for yourself") indicates for Origen that
"every sinner kindles for himself the flame of his own fire, and
is not plunged into some fire which has already been kindled by
another or existed before himself."[82] But by far the most dominant
metaphor for Origen is that of education. He sees souls as having
been created with a desire to know God. That desire is distorted
by sin. Through revelation (that is, through Christ in the incarnation and in scripture) people can come to know God by degrees;
but this process needs to be continued after death. Thus, Origen's
particular notion of punishment after death is the eschatological
outworking of his "pedagogic soteriology": what happens after
death is both punishment/correction *and* "sanctification."[83]

We can better understand the importance of pedagogy for Origen if we understand two things about education in the ancient
world. First, good education was believed then (as now) to require
the "active participation" of the subject.[84] This explains how Origen can insist that God bringing all to salvation is compatible with
human free will. Even if it takes long ages, Origen believes that all
souls will eventually willingly participate in the process of being
educated into as full a knowledge of God as possible. Second,
education in the ancient world was frequently associated with
very hard effort; self-denying discipline; and, very often, punishment (including corporal punishment). While a modern reader
might not necessarily associate punishment with education, to

81. *DP* 2.10.6.
82. *DP* 2.10.4. See also the "outer darkness" understood in terms of sinners sepa-
rating themselves from the light of God: *DP* 2.10.8. Isaiah 50:11 (LXX), in the form
quoted by Origen.
83. Greggs, "Apokatastasis," 40.
84. Greggs, "Apokatastasis," 33.

the ancient mind they were inextricable. Therefore, associating the afterlife at once with being educated by angels in schools for souls *and* with painful punishment was not holding two concepts in tension. Education and punishment, in the ancient world, were two sides of the same coin.

The consequences of a purificatory and educative concept of postmortem punishment were very significant for Christian history. On the one hand, Origen does not back away from stressing that the progress of souls after death (excepting the souls of saints) will be painful and demanding. As Tom Greggs suggests, "Origen is desirous that the future prospect of the universal salvation of Christ does not undermine a desire for the holy life in the present: indeed, it is through progress and holiness that the *apokatastasis* will take place."[85] To this extent, Origen would have reason, I think, to be disappointed—for a recurrent complaint against universalism, both his and that of others, is that it would encourage moral laxity. On the other hand, Origen's emphasis on the continuity of spiritual progress through this life and the next surely had a long and lasting effect on Christian spirituality, especially that of ascetics. At its worst, the notion could lead to a self-centered piety in which virtue is inculcated simply for one's own future good. At its best, however, it would lead to a profound spirituality based on the faith that the encounter with God in Christ is a transformative one.

Gregory of Nyssa

When compared with each other, Origen is probably more famous as a philosophical theologian and Gregory of Nyssa as a "spiritual" writer. Although this categorization is somewhat unfair, because each man has elements of both kinds of theology, it does reflect how they have been received in recent decades. However, it also to some extent reflects the way in which Gregory was

85. Greggs, "Apokatastasis," 44.

taking up and working with the theological inheritance from Origen. In his theology of postmortem transformation, Gregory vari-
ously accepts, nuances, or challenges the implications of Origen's
work, developing and integrating it more fully into a theology of
the ascetic life (broadly understood).[86]

Thus, Gregory agrees with Origen that if God punishes people
after their death, it will be for their own good. He often associ-
ates this punishment with purification, using the metaphor of the
refiner's fire from 1 Corinthians 3. For example, in his *Catechetical
Oration*, Gregory writes,

> The approach of the Divine power, acting like fire, effects the dis-
> appearance of the element which was contrary to nature, and, by
> thus purging it, benefits the nature. . . . When by these long and
> circuitous methods the evil, which is now mingled with our nature
> . . . , has been finally expelled from it, and when those who are
> now plunged in vice are restored to their original state, a chorus of
> thanksgiving will arise from all creation. . . . This . . . is contained
> in the great mystery of the divine Incarnation. For by mingling
> with humanity . . . he effected all the results we have previously
> described, delivering man from vice and healing the very author
> of vice.[87]

He stresses that punishment after death is linked with one's
participation in the offer of divine transformation in this life. In his
dialogue *On the Soul and the Resurrection*, Gregory's interlocu-
tor, Macrina, suggests that some souls are "cleansed from evil" in
this life, while others will be perfected "having afterwards in the

86. Like his fellow Cappadocians Basil of Caesarea and Gregory of Nazianzus,
Gregory of Nyssa understood asceticism as a disciplined life directed toward God
that could be undertaken by any Christian—ordained, religious, or lay, married
or single.
87. Gregory of Nyssa, *Catechetical Oration* 26, in Gregory of Nyssa, *The Catechetical Oration of Gregory of Nyssa*, trans. J. H. Srawley (Cambridge: Cambridge
University Press, 1903), 82–83.

necessary periods been cleansed by the fire."[88] This purification is sometimes seen as medicinal: "The medicine of virtue was applied to [the soul] in the present life, in order to heal such wounds. But if it remains unhealed, its cure has been provided for it in the life which follows hereafter."[89]

Possibly because he is aware of the accusation that a universal hope might encourage moral laxity, Gregory seems even more concerned to stress the difference between the transformative process now and after death. The present process is one of discipline; the later will be one of pain—pain that is described by Gregory with very vivid metaphors. In *On the Soul and the Resurrection*, for example, he compares the punishment of the soul to a rope losing the clay encrusted around it as it is pulled through a hole and to mangled bodies being pulled painfully out of earthquake-shattered buildings. Macrina's description of the fate of the soul almost dwells on the pain: "The Divine force, for God's very love of man, drags that which belongs to Him from the ruins of the irrational and material. Not in hatred or revenge for a wicked life, to my thinking, does God bring upon sinners those painful dispensations; He is only claiming and drawing to himself whatever, to please Him, came into existence. But while He for a noble end is attracting the soul to Himself, the Fountain of all Blessedness, this is necessarily the cause of a state of torture to the being which is thus attracted."[90]

Gregory's distinction between transformation now and transformation after death also seems to emphasize the role of human

88. Gregory of Nyssa, *On the Soul and the Resurrection*, in NPNF 2/5:465. See also Gregory of Nyssa, *On the Soul and the Resurrection*, in NPNF 2/5:449.

89. Gregory of Nyssa, *Catechetical Oration* 8, in Gregory of Nyssa, *Catechetical Oration*, trans. Srawley, 48.

90. Gregory of Nyssa, *On the Soul and the Resurrection*, in NPNF 2/5:451 (trans. slightly reworded). See also: "either having been purified during the present life by diligence and philosophy, or after removal from here by the purifying furnace of fire" (Gregory of Nyssa, "In Regard to Those Fallen Asleep (*De Mortuis*)," 109; GNO IX, 54.17–20).

freedom in this life: if a Christian actively participates in the transforming effects of salvation now, they will suffer less after their
death.[91] However, in some places Gregory seems to suggest that
even after death the process will be pedagogical, effecting a change
of the will toward God: "Therefore, so that this authority [i.e.,
freedom of will] might remain in human nature and evil might
pass away, God's wisdom found this device to permit humanity
to become what he wished, so that by tasting the evils it desired
and learning by experience what sort of things it had exchanged
for the kinds it chose, it might return willingly by desire to its
first blessedness."[92]

Thus far, Gregory can be understood as nuancing Origen's
position. Their conception of postmortem punishment is distinctive to early Greek Christianity, and there are clear continuities
between the two theologians. But when expanding on the idea of
the soul's development in the afterlife, Gregory develops a position
that is truly distinctive to himself. First, he describes the soul's
condition in terms that again and again have recourse to the notion of movement, and specifically of ascent. Some of his language
recalls that of the soul's ascent in the *Phaedrus* or the *Symposium*
(Gregory is fond of the motif of steps or stairs).[93] Nevertheless,
although he borrows Platonic imagery and even terminology, the
concept is thoroughly Christianized and often expressed through
close engagement with the biblical text. For example, he interprets
Moses's encounter with the darkness on Mount Sinai as a type of

91. For a fuller treatment of this, see Ludlow, *Universal Salvation*, chap. 3, sec. C,
"Universal Salvation and Human Freedom."
92. Gregory of Nyssa, "In Regard to Those Fallen Asleep (*De Mortuis*)," 109;
GNO IX, 54.11–16.
93. Morwenna Ludlow, "Divine Infinity and Eschatology: The Limits and Dy-
namics of Human Knowledge, according to Gregory of Nyssa (CE II.67–170),"
in Gregory of Nyssa, *Contra Eunomium II: An English Version with Supporting
Studies. Proceedings of the Tenth International Colloquium on Gregory of Nyssa
(Olomouc, September 15–18, 2004)*, ed. Lenka Karfíková, Scot Douglass, and Jo-
hannes Zachhuber, trans. S. G. Hall, Supplements to Vigiliae Christianae (Leiden:
Brill, 2007).

the soul's ascent to God (likewise Abraham's journey from Ur).[94] Gregory often refers to Paul's image of an athlete "straining forward" (*epekteinomenos*) for a finishing line (Phil. 3:13–14); hence his teaching of the ascent of the soul is often referred to by a term derived from this verb: *epektasis*. Gregory sees the ascent in three ways, often blending the three together: it is an ascent in knowledge; it is a moral ascent, in which the soul increases in virtue;[95] and it is an ascent in love, or an ascent through a desire for God. This last is found especially in Gregory's homilies on the Song of Songs.[96] Gregory stresses that although the soul participates in the process of ascent, it is attracted by the beauty of God (a dominant theme in his commentary on the Song of Songs) or, as he puts in in his commentary on the Beatitudes, led by the hand by Christ, through the scriptures.[97]

Put in terms of knowledge, the goal is not to know God but "to be known by God and to become someone dear to him."[98] One reason for this is the priority of divine grace over human effort. Another reason is that Gregory boldly asserts that the soul ultimately *cannot* know God. Origen had sometimes made hints in this direction, although he also stressed the eschatological vision

94. See Gregory of Nyssa, *The Life of Moses*, trans. Abraham Malherbe, The Classics of Western Spirituality (New York: Paulist Press, 1978), 2.163; Gregory of Nyssa, *Contra Eunomium II*, 2.86–96.

95. For Gregory, as for many Greek philosophers, virtue is not the condition of complying with laws or norms; rather, it is a quality of soul achieved by the habitual practice of a good life. For the moral ascent, see esp. Gregory of Nyssa, *Homilies on the Beatitudes: An English Version with Commentary and Supporting Studies. Proceedings of the Eighth International Colloquium on Gregory of Nyssa (Paderborn, September 14–18, 1998)*, trans. S. G. Hall, vol. 52, Supplements to Vigiliae Christianae (Leiden: Brill, 2000), 2.1.

96. Gregory of Nyssa, *Homilies on the Song of Songs*, trans. Richard A Norris, Writings from the Greco-Roman World (Atlanta: Society of Biblical Literature, 2012), 171 (see also Hom. 5); Gregory of Nyssa, *In Canticum Canticorum*, ed. H. Langerbeck, Gregorii Nysseni Opera VI (Leiden: Brill, 1986), 158.8. Hereafter this work is cited as GNO VI.

97. Gregory of Nyssa, *Homilies on the Beatitudes* 4.1; Gregory of Nyssa, *Homilies on the Song of Songs*, 171; GNO VI, 158.12–159.4.

98. Gregory of Nyssa, *Life of Moses* 2.320.

of God "face to face," compared to humans' present condition.[99] Other theologians had alluded to the distance between created human intellects and their creator. Gregory, however, appears to be one of the first theologians to make the philosophical claim that the divine nature is infinite, thus it would be *impossible* for a finite human mind to comprehend God.[100] While this might seem like a counsel of despair, in fact Gregory develops a doctrine of *epektasis*—or, infinite movement into God—according to which the human mind, although never fully comprehending God, is yet infinitely sustained by God's love at each step of the way. One image he uses to express this is that of the infinitely capacious cup: "Soul-receptacles with free choice were constructed like jars by the all-sustaining Wisdom so that there should be some space to receive [divine] goods, a space which always becomes bigger through the addition of what is poured into it."[101]

99. E.g., Origen, "Commentary on the Song," in *The Song of Songs: Commentary and Homilies*, trans. R. P. Lawson, Ancient Christian Writers 26 (Westminster, MD: Newman, 1957), 2.100–101, 3.183–84.

100. Anthony Meredith, "Gregory of Nyssa," in *The Cambridge History of Philosophy in Late Antiquity*, ed. Lloyd P. Gerson, vol. 1 (Cambridge: Cambridge University Press, 2010). Mark Weedman has argued against the claim that Gregory was the very first ("The Polemical Context of Gregory of Nyssa's Doctrine of Divine Infinity," *Journal of Early Christian Studies* 18, no. 1 [2010]: 81–104). See also Ekkehard Mühlenberg, *Die Unendlichkeit Gottes bei Gregor von Nyssa: Gregors Kritik am Gottesbegriff der klassischen Metaphysik* (Göttingen: Vandenhoeck & Ruprecht, 1966).

101. Gregory of Nyssa, *On the Soul and the Resurrection*, Patrologia Graeca, ed. J.-P. Migne, 161 vols. (Paris, 1857–86), 46:105A.

2

Evangelical Universalism

Robin A. Parry

I am an evangelical universalist—at least, that is how I think of myself.[1] However, in one sense I really have little interest in evangelicalism as such. What matters—and what I care about—is the *ekklēsia*, the one church of God. Evangelicalism is a social phenomenon, and in the providence of God it has had, and continues to have, something of value to contribute to the church—but it is not the church.[2]

Nevertheless, as a renewal movement within the church, with both strengths and weaknesses, evangelicalism has played an important role in the modern world. And I value my evangelical heritage.

1. See the book I originally published in 2006 (under a pseudonym), which is now in a second edition: Gregory MacDonald, *The Evangelical Universalist*, 2nd ed. (Eugene, OR: Cascade Books, 2012).
2. In ontological terms, I am a nominalist regarding evangelicalism but a realist regarding the church.

It was though this manifestation of Christianity that God laid hold of my life, and it was in this context that I was spiritually formed. I know the debt I owe, and I know that my faith will always have an evangelical shape to it.

But evangelical *universalism*? Surely that must be a bridge too far, even an oxymoron! One thing that most people think they know about evangelicals is that they believe in eternal hell (whether that be annihilation or everlasting torment). Indeed, this is something that most *evangelicals* think they know about evangelicals! And, to be fair, they are almost correct. It is certainly true to say that most evangelicals, past and present, have affirmed eternal hell. Dissent has only ever been at the margins of the movement. However, minority report though it be, dissent there has been—right from the start. What I call evangelical universalism can be traced back to the beginning of the Evangelical Revival,[3] and further back into some of the roots of that revival in late seventeenth-century Protestantism. Sure, this optimistic strand of evangelicalism has always been met with fierce opposition from within the movement itself. However, that does not necessarily disqualify it from being an evangelical option. After all, Arminianism has also been met with fierce resistance from Calvinist evangelicals (such as Jonathan Edwards), and Arminians (such as John Wesley) have returned the favor.

So, can universalism be legitimately evangelical? I maintain that it can on the grounds that (a) it is not incompatible with any central evangelical affirmations and, just as importantly, (b) it has a serious claim to arise precisely *from* central evangelical affirmations. Let me address the first of these matters briefly. (I'll come back to the second later.)

It seems to me that much of the anxiety about universal salvation in evangelical circles has usually arisen from simple misunderstandings about it. Various popular misperceptions continue to circulate,

3. In US history, the Evangelical Revival is often referred to as the First Great Awakening.

and dispelling them may take a significant amount of heat out of the discussion. Some common myths are that universalists

- overemphasize God's love, to the exclusion of justice and wrath;
- don't believe in eschatological judgment;
- reject the authority of scripture;
- don't think that sin is very bad;
- think that all roads lead to God;
- ignore evangelism; and
- have no motivation for holy living.[4]

Once the species of universalism under discussion is clarified, and it is understood that these objections do not apply to it, evangelicals are much more willing to have calm and respectful discussions. This is even more the case once it is grasped that universal restoration is perfectly compatible with core evangelical convictions: trust in the triune God; high Christology; the centrality of the incarnation and the saving work of Christ in his ministry, death, resurrection, ascension, and return; justification by grace alone, through faith alone; a high view of biblical authority; the importance of mission; and so on.[5] Of course, this growing openness

4. I have briefly addressed all these misunderstandings in "Bell's Hells: Seven Myths about Universalism," *The Baptist Times*, March 18, 2011, 8–9, and "Evangelical Universalism: Oxymoron?," *Evangelical Quarterly* 84, no. 1 (2012): 3–18. For more detail, see MacDonald, *Evangelical Universalist*.

5. The only significant traditional evangelical beliefs that universalists typically reject are (a) that death is the point after which there are no further opportunities for repentance and faith, and (b) that it is impossible to be delivered from "hell" once one is there. The question is whether these beliefs are *nonnegotiable* for evangelicals. Universalists argue that they are secondary matters and that there is scope for diverse opinions on them. Many universalists would go on to argue that the notion of death as the point of no return cannot be adequately grounded in scripture (Heb. 9:27 is perhaps the key proof text for this view, but it is compatible with opportunities for postmortem salvation) and, furthermore, that it is incompatible with other central Christian affirmations (e.g., divine love and justice). Such universalists would,

to discussion does *not* mean that wary evangelicals will embrace universalism as true; but they are increasingly open to considering it a live option in an *in-house* debate.[6] Not all will concur, and some see absolute resistance to universalism to be critical.[7] But the direction of travel, it appears to me, is toward the view that even if "evangelical universalism" is mistaken, it is not an oxymoron.

As a catholic evangelical, I should offer a word here to set this discussion in wider ecumenical context. One of the perennial temptations for evangelicals is to elevate secondary theological issues to the status of primary concerns, transforming them into matters of dogma and making those who disagree into heretics. "Heresy" is a word far too liberally deployed by some evangelicals. I think what counts as dogma or heresy should be decided by the ecumenical consensus of the church, not by individuals or denominations. This being the case, universalism, I would argue, occupies a space *between* dogma and heresy. It is certainly not something that one must embrace in order to be an orthodox Christian. To say so would be to make most Christians from the past fourteen hundred years or so into believers in heresy[8]—a move as indefensible as it is extreme. So universalism is not dogma. But neither is it something the affirmation of which would put one at odds with the faith of the church. That is to say, it is not heresy.[9] In my

---

therefore, say that the notion of death as the point of no return should be rejected. That is a discussion for another time. (And I ought to note that some evangelical universalists do not teach deliverance from "hell" as part of their theology.)

6. All reflective evangelicals understand that a view can be evangelical-compatible while at the same time being untrue. That is how premillennialists, postmillennialists, and amillennialists, say, can accept one another as evangelical while at the same time thinking one another mistaken.

7. This is evidenced, for instance, by the experiences of evangelical pastors who have been dismissed from their posts after affirming universal restoration. I know several such people. I am also familiar with several believers disfellowshipped from their churches after refusing to repudiate universal restoration.

8. Though not necessarily into heretics. To be a heretic one must not only believe something contrary to the mind of the church but also *know* that one is so doing.

9. For a discussion of this claim and of the Fifth Ecumenical Council, see Gregory MacDonald, "Introduction: Between Heresy and Dogma," in *"All Shall Be Well"*:

view, it is a *theologoumenon*: an important theological teaching, one that it is worth exploring and debating, but one about which the church is not of one mind. There is space within orthodoxy to disagree about it. Consequently, I am somewhat averse to the ambiguous term "dogmatic universalism" to describe my view. I think that "confident universalism" is much more accurate. I am confident that universal salvation is the sober truth, and I am very happy to defend it against critics, but I emphatically do *not* think that it is a theological principle above challenge or that those who deny it (i.e., most Christians) are thereby denying the faith.

That said, I do think there is a relationship between universalism and orthodoxy. It seems to me that, in spite of the accusation of heresy sometimes leveled against it, universalism is arguably more consistent with orthodox teaching than its alternatives. If one believes that God will damn some to eternal destruction (whether everlasting torment or annihilation), then one has a major challenge to show how such a belief is compatible with other claims Christians wish to make about God (e.g., that God is love, that God is "almighty," and so on). I don't have space to spell out the thinking here, but it is not hard to figure.[10] I maintain that, to date, there has been no successful attempt to demonstrate the compatibility of eternal hell with the God of the gospel. There have been plenty of attempts, but none has successfully defanged the worrisome beast. This does *not* mean that those who believe in hell are thereby denying orthodoxy. However, it does mean—or so it seems to me—that they must be content to live with beliefs that appear formally incoherent and must be prepared to come to terms with a troublesome and seemingly irresolvable tension in their faith. The bigger worry is that those who cannot live with contradiction

Explorations in Universal Salvation and Christian Theology, from Origen to Moltmann, ed. Gregory MacDonald (Eugene, OR: Cascade Books, 2011), 1–25.

10. For an instance of the reasoning spelled out, see John Kronen and Eric Reitan, *God's Final Victory: A Comparative Philosophical Case for Universalism* (New York: Bloomsbury, 2011).

but who insist on retaining hell may be tempted to start redefining some of their beliefs about God and salvation to solve the problem. Here is where a threat to orthodoxy can come into play. One of the strongest arguments for universal restoration is that it provides a compelling way of holding together certain fundamental Christian beliefs. Thus, rather than being heresy, belief in universal salvation can serve as a way of maintaining a *consistent* and *coherent* orthodoxy. (Oh, the irony!)

The Historical Roots of Evangelical Universalism

The different species of Christian universalism did not drop from heaven but emerged in specific sociohistorical contexts that informed the particular shapes they came to take on. We do not have time here to do any more than gesture at the ecclesial situations within which evangelical universalism grew,[11] but a quick glance may help us to get some bearings.

The roots of evangelical universalism are found in the European Pietist movement of the late seventeenth century and the evangelical revivals of the eighteenth century in both Britain and America. It was a popular movement, often taking place among uneducated and marginal folk. The theologians of the movement are not of the caliber of a John Wesley or a Jonathan Edwards. Nevertheless, they were not dumb, and their theological arguments still warrant serious attention.

Pietist Roots: From Europe to America and Back Again

Pietism was a renewal movement within and without German Lutheranism, an attempt to reform the Reformation.[12] Pietism was a diverse movement drawing on eclectic influences, and it included

11. Evangelical universalism is my own term, not one employed by most of those whose views I designate by it. However, it is, I think, heuristically useful.
12. See Douglas H. Shantz, *An Introduction to German Pietism* (Baltimore: Johns Hopkins University Press, 2013).

universalists among its early leaders and adherents. Here one thinks in particular of Radical Pietists like Johann Wilhelm Petersen (1649–1726) and his wife Johanna (1644–1724).[13] Johann had become a universalist in 1694 under the influence of an English mystic called Jane Leade (1624–1704).[14] Petersen became an eager promoter of the message of *Wiederbringung aller Dinge* (restoration of all things) in both his preaching and his writing ministry. He traveled widely in German lands and was a prolific author.[15] This message was not well received by all Pietists, especially in Halle, but it did gather an audience. According to Petersen, Philipp Jakob Spener (1635–1705) himself—one of the major figures of Pietism—while not speaking out publicly for or against universal restoration, privately confided that he hoped that it was so.

There were a number of universalist and millenarian Radical Pietist groups and itinerant preachers in this period, ministering not only in Germany but in France and the Netherlands. One group even produced their own new translation of the Bible—the Berleburg Bible (1726). When the political situation turned against them in the early eighteenth century, many thousands migrated to America. One such group was the German Baptists (or Dunkers), though they preferred to be called Brethren. They were largely believers in universal salvation, and some of their number were proactive in spreading the message in the "new world."

One of those who moved to America and settled among the German Baptists was George de Benneville (1703–93).[16] His own

13. See Shantz, *Introduction to German Pietism*, 159–66; Johanna Petersen, *The Life of Lady Johanna Eleonora Petersen, Written by Herself* (Chicago: University of Chicago Press, 2005).

14. See Julie Hirst, *Jane Leade: Biography of a Seventeenth-Century Mystic* (Aldershot, UK: Ashgate, 2005).

15. Petersen has about 150 works attributed to him. His wife, Johanna, published fifteen.

16. See George de Benneville, *A True and Most Remarkable Account of Some Passages in the Life of Mr. George de Benneville*, trans. Elhanan Winchester (London, 1791); Albert Bell, *The Life and Times of Dr. George de Benneville (1703–1793)* (Boston: The Universalist Church of America, 1953).

story is fascinating: He was the son of aristocratic Huguenot
refugees who fled to England, where he was brought up in the
court of Queen Anne. As a teenager, a religious experience of
God's love for all his creatures led de Benneville away from his
childhood Calvinism to a belief that God would save all. He took
up working as a preacher in Europe, and he was within a gnat's
whisker of being executed in France before a last-minute pardon
from the king. Undeterred, he continued preaching the "everlasting gospel" far and wide. A visionary experience, when he was
close to death from an illness, further reinforced his universalism.
When he moved to America, de Benneville settled in Pennsylvania,
working as a doctor and a teacher and continuing his itinerant
preaching. Perhaps of more lasting influence than his preaching
was his instigation of the translation (from German into English)
and the publication of a universalist book by Paul Siegvolck,[17]
The Everlasting Gospel. This book had some impact across the
American colonies, with one of its most significant converts being
a man named Elhanan Winchester (1751–97).[18]

Winchester was a New England Congregationalist who converted in a New Light revival and then became an evangelical
Baptist. He ministered as a revivalist preacher and a Baptist minister, serving in New England and South Carolina before moving
to become pastor at the important First Baptist Church of Philadelphia. However, unknown to his congregation, Winchester had
been wrestling for some while with the case for universal restoration, having come across Siegvolck's book while he was in South
Carolina. Not long after accepting the position in Philadelphia, he

17. A pseudonym for Georg Klein-Nicolai, a German universalist. The book was
published in German in 1705 and translated into English in 1753, perhaps by de
Benneville himself. Elhanan Winchester published an edition in London in 1792.

18. On Winchester, see Robin Parry, "The Baptist Universalist: Elhanan Winchester (1751–97)," http://www.academia.edu/8643336/_The_Baptist_Universalist
_Elhanan_Winchester_1751_97. See also Nathan A. Finn, "The Making of a Baptist
Universalist: The Curious Case of Elhanan Winchester," *Baptist History & Heritage*
47 (Fall 2012): 6–18.

became convinced from the Bible that God would save all people. This created a crisis in the church, and Winchester and his followers were forced out, forming the Universal Baptists. He met with de Benneville, who was based in Germantown,[19] just north of Philadelphia, and occasionally went on preaching tours with him. Winchester began a successful ministry as an evangelical universalist minister and preacher in America, based in Philadelphia, and then for a few years in London (1778–94), before returning to the United States in 1794. His influential message was a blend of the Pietistic mode of universal restoration and the mode of the evangelical revivals, and he left his impact on both America and Britain—particularly among nonconformists. Even more influential than his preaching were his publications—in particular, his work *The Universal Restoration* (1788). This is one of the classic works of the early universalist movement and reflects deep evangelical sensibilities.

From 1735, another Continental pietistic stream that brought universalism to America was the Moravians.[20] It is likely that Count von Zinzendorf (1700–1760), the great man behind the Moravian mission movement of the third wave of Pietism, was a universalist. In his *Sixteen Discourses*, Zinzendorf writes, "By His [Christ's] Name, all can *and shall* obtain life and salvation."[21] Certainly some, albeit a minority, of the early Moravian missionaries believed in the salvation of all. One such was Peter Böhler (1712–75), who was sent by Zinzendorf to the Americas, where he was active in spreading the gospel and was a key leader in the movement in both America and Britain. His universalism was clearly not something that dampened his missional passion.

19. Germantown had been purchased by Johanna and Johann Petersen, both Radical Pietists with universalist convictions, and was populated by many with similar convictions.

20. I am grateful to Professor John Coffey for alerting me to universalism amongst the Moravians.

21. Nicolaus Zinzendorf, *Sixteen Discourses on the Redemption of Man by the Death of Christ* (London: James Hutton, 1740), 30, emphasis added.

The fact that Zinzendorf and Peter Böhler believed (and sometimes taught) a doctrine of universal restoration was one of many
idiosyncrasies that undid their relationship with Whitefield, Wesley, and Dutch and American Reformed evangelicals. Wesley expressed concern to Zinzendorf about the universalism in the latter's *Sixteen Discourses*,[22] and the Dutch Reformed condemned
Zinzendorf for it. Whitefield wrote to Wesley in 1740 that Peter
Böhler, whom Wesley regarded highly, had told him that "all the
damned souls would hereafter be brought out of hell" and advanced this "in order to make out universal redemption."[23] Likewise, Gilbert Tennent's *Some Account of the Principles of the
Moravians*[24] repeatedly alleges that Zinzendorf and his lieuten-
ants, like August Spangenberg (1704–92), taught or at least implied
universal restoration.[25]

Revival Roots: From Britain to America

Several springs of universalism opened up in eighteenth-century
Britain that intersected in different ways with the evangelical revival.
One thinks, for instance, of Sir George Stonehouse (d. 1793), a
member of the Holy Club in Oxford (1729–35), alongside George
Whitefield and the Wesley brothers. Stonehouse was a gifted scholar
(authoring a Syriac grammar), a friend of Zinzendorf, an Anglican

22. John Wesley's *The Works of the Rev John Wesley*, vol. 2 (London: Jones, 1809), 106.
23. George Whitefield, *George Whitefield's Journals* (Edinburgh: Banner of Truth, 1986), 587.
24. Gilbert Tennent, *Some Account of the Principles of the Moravians* (London: Mason, 1743).
25. After Zinzendorf's death, Spangenberg worked hard to rehabilitate the Moravians in the eyes of wider evangelicalism, and his influential *A Concise Historical Account of the Present Constitution of the Unitas Fratrum: or, Unity of the Evangelical
Brethren, Who Adhere to the Augustan Confession* (1775), detailing the Moravian
missions, presented a conventional doctrine of hell. Any early universalism within the
movement was airbrushed out, though it is still striking that Spangenberg's summary
of Moravian gospel preaching begins, not with our sin and God's wrath, but with
the statement "God loves you." (70).

cleric, and a staunch defender of the salvation of all. The issue
was discussed at the Holy Club, and many years later Stonehouse
published his reflections in a learned study entitled *Universal Restitution, a Scripture Doctrine* (1761), a book that later shaped
Elhanan Winchester's universalism. He was distressed that John
Wesley refused to engage the book, and this spurred him to pen
two further universalist publications.

Early evangelicalism was also influenced by other universalists, including the Pietists and Moravians (see above) and the Anglican cleric and mystic William Law (1686–1761).[26] Law, whom
John Wesley, among others, held in high esteem, was not a rabid
preacher of universalism, but he clearly affirmed it.[27]

More contentious was James Relly (1722–78). Relly was a Welsh
convert of the great evangelist George Whitefield, and for nine
years he worked as one of Whitefield's itinerant gospel preachers
(1741–50).[28] However, a theological crisis regarding the justice of
God in punishing an innocent person (Christ) on behalf of others led him to develop his own idiosyncratic version of Calvinist
universalism. Relly built everything around the notion of Christ's
union with his people and theirs with him. The ontological nature
of the union meant that Christ was not some innocent third party,
as far as human sin was concerned, but participated in our guilt,
though he himself was sinless. As such, he could pay the price for
our sin. And our union with him is such that we participate in his
resurrection life. Relly believed that scripture teaches the union of
all humanity with Christ, and so he believed that *all humans are*

26. Law was an admirer of the German mystic Jakob Böhme. Böhme was a direct
influence on various universalists at the time: the Philadelphians (a late seventeenth-
century British end-times sect with universalist beliefs, guided by the pneumatic visions of Jane Leade), the Pietists, and Thomas Erskine, among others. John Murray,
however, thought Böhme and his admirers befuddled.

27. See, e.g., Law's *Affectionate and Earnest Address to the Clergy* (London,
1761), addresses 191 and 192.

28. On Relly, see Wayne K. Clymer, "Union with Christ: The Calvinist Universalism of James Relly (1722–1778)," in MacDonald, *"All Shall Be Well,"* 116–40.

already redeemed. The price has been paid for them, and so they are free. However, ignorance of this truth leads to many psychological sufferings associated with believing oneself sold into sin and guilt. The gospel message proclaims the truth and sets people free to enjoy the salvation that is already theirs in Christ.

Relly's message caused a split with Whitefield, and even more so with Whitefield's followers, who hated Relly, accusing him of antinomianism. He became an Independent minister in London (1757–78) and preached his uncompromising message in the face of opposition from Calvinists and Arminians alike. Relly's book *Union* (1759), in which he expounded his teaching on union with Christ, was highly impactful.[29] Perhaps even more significant, however, was Relly's indirect influence through the ministry of one of his converts, John Murray.

John Murray (1741–1815) was brought up as an Anglican with Methodist leanings and knew both Wesley and Whitefield.[30] It was Whitefield's Calvinistic Methodism to which he was most drawn, and he joined Whitefield's congregation in London. Like the rest of the congregation, he had regarded Relly as a devil. But in an attempt to win back a woman who had been seduced by Relly's theology, he was horrified to find himself out-argued. Eventually, he himself came to embrace what he liked to call "the truth as it is in Jesus," and for the rest of his life he was a devoted Rellyan. "The foundation of my sentiments, which appears to me to be so well laid, as to be strictly speaking immovable, is that God is unchangeable; that he never loves at one time what he hates at another; that he is the irrevocable *foe of sin, and the never varying*

29. James Relly, *Union: Or a Treatise of the Consanguinity and Affinity between Christ and His Church* (London, 1759). His more explicitly universalist teachings can be found in his *Epistles: Or, The Great Salvation Contemplated; in a Series of Letters to a Christian Society* (London: Lewis, 1776).

30. See Murray's fascinating autobiography, completed by his wife after his death: *Records of the Life of Rev. John Murray, Late Minister of Reconciliation, and Senior Pastor of the Universalists, Congregated in Boston* (Boston: Munroe & Francis, 1816).

friend of the sinner."[31] Murray made a Rellyan terminological distinction—inconsistently applied—between redemption and salvation. *All are already redeemed* from eternal divine retribution because Christ has paid the price for all, but *all are not yet saved* from the griefs that are consequent upon sin. In light of the cross, the torments of sinners, now and postmortem, are not retributive but, rather, the natural outworking of sin. This Rellyan scheme seemed to most universalists at the time to be inadequate, as it has to most universalists since.

Murray immigrated to America in 1770 to get away from his life in England, which had been marked by multiple tragedies. He unexpectedly found himself invited to preach in various places, and he eventually became the pastor of a small gathering of Rellyan believers in Gloucester, Massachusetts. This became the first official universalist church in America (though not the first universalist group). From here, and later from Boston, where he was a pastor for many years, he launched a grueling itinerant preaching ministry, spreading the universalist message of James Relly far and wide.[32] Murray is considered by many to be the father of American universalism, though this underestimates the contributions of others to the establishing of the early movement.

Revival Roots: Homegrown American Revivalist Universalism

In addition to the importation of Continental and British forms of universalism, America also witnessed the rise of its own homegrown brand of evangelical universalism, stemming from the Great Awakening.[33] The born-again saints of the revival

31. John Murray, *Letters and Sketches of Sermons*, vol. 1 (Boston: Belcher, 1812), 161.

32. Many of his sermons were published by his wife in *Letters and Sketches of Sermons*, 3 vols. They are instructive, albeit somewhat hermeneutically idiosyncratic. A large part of many of his sermons is simple citations from the Bible, for Murray liked to think he was allowing the Bible to speak for itself.

33. On American universalism, see Stephen A. Marini, *Radical Sects of Revolutionary New England* (Cambridge: Harvard University Press, 1982).

were divided between those who sought to renew New England Congregationalism from within (the so-called New Lights,[34] like Jonathan Edwards) and those individuals and whole congregations who sought a more radical solution—breaking away from Congregationalism, though still deeply influenced by it, and setting up new groups in which they could pursue their own "pure" revivalist faith. One of these radical revivalist groups was universalist in orientation, beginning in the early 1770s and focused in the hill country of rural New England. Its leaders included Isaac Davis (ca. 1700–1777), Adams Streeter (1735–86), and Caleb Rich (1750–1821).

Isaac Davis separated from Congregationalism and, in the 1770s, published a universalist treatise entitled *What Love Jesus Christ Has for Sinners*. He gathered a small community around him, known as Davisonians. He was perhaps the first New England universalist. Adams Streeter, a fellow Separatist and later a Baptist elder, was converted to universalism in 1777, perhaps under Isaac Davis's influence. Streeter was an important preacher and shaper of the early movement. More important, however, was Caleb Rich, a man with deep Calvinist roots who was led to annihilationism through a series of visions in 1772. As a result, he was expelled from Warwick Baptist Church for heresy and set up his own "religious society" in 1773. This grew into several flourishing congregations in New Hampshire. A further charismatic episode—a visitation from a celestial visitor in 1778—corrected the error of Rich's annihilationism and turned him toward an all-encompassing salvation. (The charismatic dimension of Rich's faith was not unique in radical revivalist evangelicalism in New England.) Rich then began to fearlessly proclaim a universalist gospel, which he considered to have been directly revealed to him by God. It was through Rich's preaching that the Baptist Hosea Ballou (1771–1852) was led to embrace salvation for all, and Ballou

34. The Old Lights being the anti-revival Congregationalists.

would become the most influential theologian and leader of the nineteenth-century Universalist denomination.[35]

John Murray and Elhanan Winchester ministered universalism in the towns and cities, but the rural hinterland belonged to the likes of Davis, Streeter, and Rich. However, the three streams (Rellyan, Continental, and homegrown) discovered one another and sought to work together from early on. There were frictions and problems, as their different versions of the faith were not fully compatible, and the universalists tended to be fierce individualists. But by the end of the century, they had united into a coalition.[36]

The Calvinist context of Congregationalist New England left an indelible stamp on universalism as it developed in America— both in what was retained and what was rejected. There was a continued affirmation of divine sovereignty, the efficacy of Christ's death, and the final eschatological victory. Yet there was a rejection of a limited election and a limited atonement. Much of Relly's message resonated well in such a context. In many ways, the self-understanding of universalism in this period was captured by the title of a 1796 tract written by the Congregationalist Joseph Huntingdon: *Calvinism Improved*.[37]

35. It was Ballou who, in the early nineteenth century, redirected the entire denomination with astonishing speed away from trinitarian theology to unitarian theology, much to John Murray's dismay. See Russell E. Miller, *The Larger Hope: The First Century of the Universalist Church in America, 1770–1870* (Boston: Unitarian Universalist Association, 1979), chap. 6.

36. Following Russell Miller, we might see 1785 as the first official appearance of universalism as a "sect" and 1794 as the start of universalism as a denomination. Miller, *Larger Hope*, chap. 4. See also Ann Lee Bressler, *The Universalist Movement in America, 1770–1880* (New York: Oxford University Press, 2001).

37. It should be noted that, for reasons of space, we have not considered various American universalists that may be found among the Episcopalians (e.g., John Tyler) and the Congregationalists (e.g., Charles Chauncey), whose stories also fed into the bigger story. On these American universalists, see Richard Eddy, *Universalism in America: A History*, vol. 1 (Boston: Universalist Publishing House, 1891), chap. 1. Chauncey was no evangelical, but his *The Mystery Hid from Ages and Generations, Made Manifest by the Gospel-Revelation* (London, 1784) is one of the most scholarly attempts from this period to explore biblical texts on universal restoration. (Jonathan

The Legacy of Early Evangelical Universalism

The denomination that was created from the convergence of the followers of Winchester, Murray, Streeter, and others very quickly moved away from its evangelical roots, at least in certain respects. It continued to hold biblical teaching to be authoritative, but it increasingly emphasized the importance of rational religion[38] and—in its misplaced Protestant disdain for tradition—moved away from its trinitarian roots and toward unitarianism and accompanying deviant Christologies (modalism, Arianism, etc.).[39] We need to recall that early evangelicalism (indeed, Protestantism more generally) was a movement that, at its fringes, was always teetering on the edge of heterodoxy, and often fell over into it.

The same shift happened in Britain under the leadership of Winchester's successor, Rev. William Vidler (1758–1816). Vidler was a Particular Baptist minister who had become a universalist through Winchester's influence. He took over the London congregation when Winchester returned to the United States, but he then converted to unitarianism and took the church in that direction, splitting the congregation. The remaining congregation increasingly departed from its evangelical roots, and all that remains of it now is a secular humanist organization. In that respect, the *evangelical* heirs to this eighteenth-century movement are found

Edwards published a response in 1789.) And it was certainly read and appreciated by evangelical universalists like Winchester.

38. Universalists were increasingly critical of evangelical revivalist culture, which they saw as bypassing rationality and manipulating people for cynical ends. See Bressler, *Universalist Movement in America*, 62–69.

39. On the history of denominational universalism in America in the nineteenth century, see Richard Eddy, *Universalism in America*, 2 vols. (Boston: Universalist Publishing House, 1891); Miller, *Larger Hope*; Bressler, *Universalist Movement in America*. We need to appreciate that the move from trinitarian to unitarian theology, not uncommon in the seventeenth to nineteenth centuries, was not motivated by "liberalism" (at least to start with), nor by universalism, but by a strong commitment to scripture accompanied by an Enlightenment rejection of the authority of tradition in favor of the individual's reason. (Remember that all the patristic universalists were deeply trinitarian.)

not in its *direct* descendants (the denominational Universalists[40])
but in those later evangelicals who found their convictions con-
verging on a belief in universal restoration. This was usually a case
of convergent evolution, rather than direct descent. Never again
would universalism be an organized movement within, albeit at
the margins of, the evangelical fold.[41] Instead, it tended to be a
matter of a few individuals rediscovering the view for themselves
and influencing other individuals via a rather complex web of
social and literary interconnections (and now numerous online
connections). Thus, such believers could be found across all the
different streams of evangelicalism: Reformed, Lutheran, Anglican, Anabaptist, Presbyterian, Baptist, Quaker, Pietist, Moravian,
Methodist, Brethren, Independent, Pentecostal, Charismatic, and
so on. Some of the better-known nineteenth-century names would
include Hannah Whitall Smith (Quaker/Holiness), Andrew Jukes
(Independent), Samuel Cox (Baptist), Thomas Erskine (Anglican),
and Johann Christoph Blumhardt (Lutheran).[42]

The twentieth century saw evangelical theology of hell contract
to exclude anything other than the mainstream view of eternal
torment, but the inevitable return of evangelical annihilationism
(revived from its nineteenth-century heyday[43]) opened the door
a crack for universalism. Three books that have pushed on the

40. Or the Unitarian Universalists, since the merger of the two denominations in 1961. The modern denomination is, for the most part, theologically liberal.
41. Though I would be remiss not to mention the tiny group of churches in Appalachia known as Primitive Baptist Universalists, or "No-Hellers." See Howard Dorgan, *In the Hands of a Happy God: The "No-Hellers" of Central Appalachia* (Knoxville: University of Tennessee Press, 1997).
42. It is also worth noting the many universalists who would not have self-identified as evangelical but whose theology and praxis resonated in many ways with evangelicals (e.g., George MacDonald, Thomas Allin, Jacques Ellul, William Barclay, Mathias Rissi, and Jürgen Moltmann). There were also evangelicals or those close to evangelicalism who did not consider themselves to be universalists but whose theology sailed very close to the wind in that regard (e.g., P. T. Forsyth, Karl Barth, T. F. Torrance, Donald Bloesch, and Miroslav Volf).
43. On which, see Christopher M. Date et al., eds., *Rethinking Hell: Readings in Evangelical Conditionalism* (Eugene, OR: Cascade Books, 2014).

opening door and generated some discussion within evangelical circles in the twenty-first century are Thomas Talbott's *The
Inescapable Love of God* (1999; 2nd ed. 2014); *Universal Salvation? The Current Debate* (2003), which is a debate book in
which Talbott engages evangelical interlocutors;[44] and Gregory
MacDonald's *The Evangelical Universalist* (2006; 2nd ed. 2012).
These have been accompanied by a host of other books and online
articles, posts, and discussion forums defending similar stances.[45]
A key turning point in the profile of the discussion came with the
publication of Rob Bell's *Love Wins* (2011).[46] Bell's book explored
a form of hopeful universalism, and this was sufficiently controversial, given Bell's high profile in American evangelicalism, to
cause a firestorm. Suddenly, universalism was an "issue" in the
mainstream. This was followed by Kevin Miller's documentary
movie *Hellbound?* (2012)[47]—released in cinemas, then on DVD
and streaming services—which further opened up the question in
evangelical churches. This exploration has gained confidence from
the growing realization that many of the early church fathers believed in the salvation of all.[48] What once seemed clearly heretical
to evangelicals no longer looks that way to a small-but-growing
number in their ranks.

44. Robin Parry and Christopher Partridge, eds., *Universal Salvation? The Current
Debate* (Grand Rapids: Eerdmans, 2003).
45. Among the better known are books by Nik Ansell, Sharon L. Baker, Jan Bonda,
Heath Bradley, Gerry Beauchemin, Doug Campbell, Jason Goroncy, Tom Greggs,
Peter Hiett, Brad Jersak (now Orthodox), Alvin Kimel (now Orthodox), Carlton Pearson, and Mathias Rissi. One especially influential online article, posted in the 1990s,
was Keith DeRose's "Universalism and the Bible." Also of note are the Tentmaker
website set up by Gary Amirault, the discussion forum www.evangelicaluniversalist
.com, and blog posts by Richard Beck and David Congdon. But these are just the
tip of the iceberg.
46. Rob Bell, *Love Wins: A Book About Heaven, Hell, and the Fate of Every
Person Who Ever Lived* (San Francisco: HarperOne, 2011).
47. *Hellbound?*, written and directed by Kevin Miller, Kevin Miller XI Productions
Inc., 2012, www.hellboundthemovie.com.
48. On which, see now Ilaria Ramelli, *The Christian Doctrine of Apokatastasis:
A Critical Assessment from the New Testament to Eriugena*, Supplements to Vigiliae
Christianae 120 (Leiden: Brill, 2013).

The Evangelical Universalist Quadrilateral

It is now time to deliver on my earlier promise to show how universal salvation arises naturally from evangelical faith. The challenge in making sense of the "evangelical" designation in "evangelical universalism" is clarifying what it is that makes evangelicalism a distinct movement within Christianity when, on the one hand, the movement itself embraces such diversity and, on the other, there is probably no "evangelical" belief or practice that one cannot also find some nonevangelical Christians embracing. This challenge has become even more difficult in recent decades, as Western evangelicalism has grown ever more diverse in its beliefs and practices, and the boundary between what is evangelical and what is not has grown more and more fuzzy.

I will be following David Bebbington in maintaining that while there are deep roots connecting evangelicalism to the Reformation and Puritanism, evangelicalism as a movement within Protestant Christianity can be traced back to the evangelical revivals of the early eighteenth century. Bebbington influentially identified four common features of evangelicalism as a transdenominational movement:[49]

- crucicentrism
- biblicism
- conversionism
- activism

It seems to me that these very same features can help us pick out some of the common aspects of evangelical universalism.

Crucicentrism

Speaking theologically and normatively, not simply descriptively, evangelical universalism is *evangel*-ical first and foremost

49. David Bebbington, *Evangelicalism in Modern Britain: A History from 1730s to 1980s* (London: Routledge, 1988), 2–3.

because it is *grounded in the evangel*, the gospel. I cannot stress this too much. It is evangelical because it accords with—more than that, because it grows from and is deeply rooted in—the gospel itself. Hence, many eighteenth-century proponents referred to their message simply as "the everlasting gospel."

The cross is core to this gospel message, hence crucicentrism. However, the cross cannot be isolated from incarnation, resurrection, and ascension—with which it forms a seamless garment. I wish to discuss it in that wider context.

The gospel is the proclamation that the triune God of Israel has been true to his covenant and has sent Jesus, the Messiah, to reveal the divine love and, through his life, death, resurrection, and ascension, to accomplish God's saving work. The good news is that Jesus succeeded—he died for our sin, and God raised him from the dead—and that he is exalted as Lord of the cosmos. The gospel proclamation demands an appropriate response—trust in him, bow your knee to him as Lord, and offer him your whole-hearted loving praise—and promises eternal life in the Spirit to all who so respond.

In the history of Israel, God revealed himself in many and various ways, but his supreme self-revelation comes in the incarnation of the divine Logos as Jesus, the Messiah (Heb. 1:1–3). The divine revelation in Christ serves to reframe and reconfigure all prior divine revelations, being their fulfillment and interpretive key. When we discuss creation, we do so in the light of Christ; when we ponder end times, we do so in the light of Christ. The gospel is protology; the gospel is eschatology. Similarly, our understanding of the God of Israel cannot be the same after the incarnation. The gospel revelation is *theo*logically loaded, giving our theology a Christocentric, trinitarian shape. It is also a revelation of human be-ing, the nature of sin, salvation, election, and so on. One cannot adequately understand the biblical metanarrative of creation to new creation without making Jesus the center.

Creation, Eschatology, and the Cross

What we see in Christ is God's way with his creation: the Father comes to and acts in the world *through* the Son, *in* the Spirit. Likewise, the world comes to the Father, *through* the Son, and *in* the Spirit. That is the economic shape of the God-world relationship. Now, in the widest scheme of things, we can speak of protology and teleology as *exitus et reditus*: all things are "from" God and are destined to return "to" God. "For from him and through him and to him are all things" (Rom. 11:36 ESV).[50] Both the *exitus* and the *reditus* have a trinitarian shape: in creation all things come *from* the Father, *through* the Son, *in* the Spirit; in the end, all things return *to* the Father, *through* the Son, *in* the Spirit.

Creation is not simply a doctrine about the past—something that happened way back when. Creation implies a goal, a purpose, a telos, a destination. God created all things *for* something. Creation is "from him" and "through him" and "*to him.*" So eschatology is implicit in the notion of creation: the universe was made for God and finds its destiny in God. And notice the universality of this claim: "*all* things" are from God and to God. In the gospel, we also see that both the "from God" and the "to God" are mediated "through God." All things were made *through* the Logos, the Son, the second person of the Trinity (John 1:1–3; Heb. 1:2; Col. 1:16, etc.). And all things (i.e., all created things) return to God *through* the mediation of this same Son, reversing Adam's transgression (Rom. 5:15–19). So the widest context for understanding the cross is that of the *reditus* mediated by the second person of the Trinity: "For in him [the Son] all things were created: things in heaven and on earth, visible and invisible, whether thrones or powers or rulers or authorities; all things have been created through him and for him. . . . For God was pleased to have all his fullness dwell in him, and through him to reconcile to himself all things, whether things on earth or things

---

50. Unless otherwise indicated, Bible quotations in this chapter are from the NIV.

in heaven, *by making peace through his blood, shed on the cross*"
(Col. 1:16–20).

Eschatology is also reconfigured by and understood aright
in light of the gospel, and eschatological claims must be tested
against the evangel. Eschatology is what we must say about the
end if God is to be the God of the gospel.[51] So, if the gospel reveals
and determines the shape of the future, what will the future look
like? And what won't it look like?

The cross, resurrection, and ascension are eschatology.[52] On
the cross, we see sin and judgment and curse and exile and death
experienced in climactic form by Jesus, our representative, participating in our brokenness, standing in our place. In the resurrection, we see the final defeat of death, the final resurrection of
the dead, and eternal life in the person of Christ. His death is
not simply his death, but the final death of humanity in him; his
resurrection is not simply his resurrection, but the resurrection of
humanity in him; his ascension to reign at God's right hand is not
simply his ascension, but the ascension of humanity in him. The
gospel *is* eschatology—it is about the coming of the kingdom of
God through Christ. And what do we see in that narrative about
the shape of the human future? Resurrection. Pneumatic life. Ascension. Universal salvation is ultimately grounded in the death
and resurrection of Christ for all humanity.

Here is why I think evangelical universalism should be a form of
confident universalism, as opposed to tentative or wishful universalism. Many theologians argue that while God *may* save all (and, of
course, they hope that he does), it would be presumptuous to say
that he *will*. Why presumptuous? Perhaps because God is sovereign

51. Here I am playing off an insight of John A. T. Robinson.
52. Indeed, the incarnation and ministry of Jesus are also eschatology. This is acknowledged in the season of Advent, when Christ's first and second comings are fused
and anticipated. That liturgical instinct reflects a profound theological insight—that
Christ's first and second advents are not two completely different and disconnected
events but two phases of a *single*, eschatological, divine advent.

and is free to do what he likes.[53] It is not for us to demand that he must behave in a certain way in the end. The evangelical universalist will be unimpressed with this line of reasoning. God is certainly free, but God's free choice regarding creation's destiny has *already been manifest in the gospel*.[54] This is not about humans telling God what he has to do in order to measure up to some standard of goodness external to the divine being—there is no such standard. Postulating a final, global salvation is not arrogant human presumption but rather a humble acknowledgment of God's gracious revelation of the future of the world in Christ. Consequently, to evangelical universalists, to imagine a different end—an end in which the tomb, rather than the resurrection, was the eternal destiny of many people—would be to imagine an end in which God had failed or had changed his mind and abandoned the gospel in order to pursue a different plan. This is theological suicide at so many levels.

An eschatology in which hell—alienation from God—is a permanent feature seems to me to be an eschatology in which something other than the gospel is calling the shots. It is an eschatology in which a significant part of the eternal pattern of things to come is determined not by divine grace but by sin and evil—a future in which a significant part of creation fails to reach the end for which God created it, in which Christ's death and resurrection are ineffectual for many of those for whom he died. Indeed, with everlasting torment God must act to perpetuate sin and evil, albeit quarantined in hell, forever and ever, rather than annihilating it. Putting it mildly, that would be shocking.

53. An alternative rationale is that human freedom will determine who participates in salvation and who does not, and such choices are, by necessity, out of God's hands. That is why we cannot know that all will be saved. This common approach seems to me riddled with problems.

54. And divine freedom must not be understood in some voluntarist way, according to which divine will is elevated above divine being such that God can will *absolutely anything*. Such a view, I think, is profoundly problematic (and unbiblical). God is free in the sense that God is absolutely free to be Godself, and nothing outside of God can compromise that freedom.

And down our throats this lie is cramm'd
Let sin be sav'd, the sinners damn'd.[55]

As annihilationists point out, there is a better end: one in which
evil is utterly removed from creation. However, annihilationists
envisage this in terms of the total destruction of *sinners*—the guil-
lotine replacing the prison. But if God were to annihilate sinners,
this would amount to sin *forever* thwarting God's purposes. It
would be God *giving up* on his mission of reconciling the world
to himself. There is a more *evangel*ical end to the story: one in
which God annihilates *sin and evil*, not sinners, from creation.
That is the ending universalists proclaim.

The Cross and Divine Love

The gospel reconfigures everything, including our understanding
of God. Take divine love. Evangelical universalists are often accused
of reading a sentimental understanding of love into the Bible. We
allegedly take our understanding of "love" from worldly wisdom,
not from scripture, and then project it onto God. This criticism
is unfair. We do not deduce the nature of God's love simply by
reflecting on ourselves. Rather, it is in the biblical story of God's
way with Israel and, supremely, in the Bible's gospel climax that
we discover *that* God is love and the *shape* of God's love. Consider,
for instance, how in 1 John the claim that "God is love"—love in
his very essence—is expounded in terms of the cross: "Anyone who
does not love does not know God, because *God is love*. In this the
love of God was made manifest among us, that God sent his only
Son into the world, so that we might live through him. In this is
love, not that we have loved God but that he loved us and sent his
Son to be the propitiation for our sins" (1 John 4:8–10 ESV).

The cross—that is how we know *that* God loves us and how
we begin to grasp what divine love *means*. Notice too that the

55. Murray, *Letters and Sketches*, 1:62.

cross is seen as the definitive manifestation of divine love *for the whole world*: "He [Jesus] is the propitiation for our sins, and not for ours only but also for the sins of the whole world" (1 John 2:2 ESV). Remember that, in Johannine literature, "the world" is the wicked, rebellious, God-hating world. So, the Johannine claim that "God is love" is explicitly connected to God's cross-shaped love for *all* people. We see this in John's Gospel too: "For God so loved the world, that he gave his only Son, that whoever believes in him should not perish but have eternal life. For God did not send his Son into the world to condemn the world, but in order that the world might be saved through him" (John 3:16–17 ESV). *Who* did God love? The sinful world that rejected him (not merely an elect subset of that world). *How* did God love the world? By sending his Son to die for its redemption.

The apostle Paul too reconfigures his understanding of love around the gospel story. "But God demonstrates his own love for us in this: While we were still sinners, Christ died for us" (Rom. 5:8). Michael Gorman thus talks of Paul's notion of *cruciform* love.[56] The contention of the universalist is that it is precisely this gospel-shaped understanding of divine love, not fuzzy sentimentalism, that motivates resistance to traditional theologies of hell.

Calvinism, Arminianism, and the Cross

One of the springs of the eighteenth-century rise in evangelical universalism that deserves highlighting is the inner-evangelical debate between Calvinists and Arminians. Universalism was thought of by its defenders as a powerful way of affirming the true insights of both sides of this debate. This is explained well by Elhanan Winchester. For Winchester, the theo-logic of the issue forces a choice between Calvinism, Arminianism, and universal restoration: "Either God created some to be miserable to endless ages

---

56. See esp. Michael Gorman, *Cruciformity: Paul's Narrative Spirituality of the Cross* (Grand Rapids: Eerdmans, 2001), 155–267.

[Calvinism], or must be frustrated eternally in his designs [Arminianism], or all must be restored at last [Universalism]."[57] One of the appeals of universalism to Winchester was that it offered a way to affirm and hold together key aspects of both the Calvinist and the Arminian systems—"to embrace them [both] in one grand system of benevolence."[58] He articulates this most clearly in his sermon *The Outcasts Comforted*.[59] We can summarize his theological points in the table below.

Doctrine	Calvinism	Arminianism	Universalism
God loves all		✓	✓
The objects of God's love will come to salvation	✓		✓
God desires to save all		✓	✓
All God's purposes will be accomplished	✓		✓
Christ died for all		✓	✓
All for whom Christ died will be saved (his blood was not shed in vain)	✓		✓

Universalist Baptists, he argues, simply affirm beliefs that mainstream Protestants hold, so they should not be considered heretical. A particular blend of certain mainstream evangelical views generates a chemical reaction that yields a universalist cocktail. A shot of Wesley mixed and shaken with a dash of Whitefield makes a Winchester.

As Winchester saw it, the problems generated within both the Calvinist and the Arminian systems stem from the conviction of

57. Elhanan Winchester, *The Universal Restoration: Exhibited in a Series of Dialogues between a Minister and His Friend* (1788; 2nd ed., London: Gillet, 1792), sec. 2, ans. 3. Hereafter this work is cited as *UR*.

58. *UR*, sec. 2, ans. 3.

59. Elhanan Winchester, *The Outcasts Comforted: A Sermon Delivered at the University of Philadelphia, January 4, 1782* (Philadelphia: Towne, 1782).

those on both sides of that divide that a belief in eternal torment is nonnegotiable. Making eternal hell a first principle requires them to sacrifice other doctrines to accommodate it. Thus Calvinists must surrender the beliefs that God loves all people deeply, that God desires to save them, and that Christ died for them. And Arminians must surrender the belief that, in the end, God will achieve all his purposes for creation, believing instead in God's *partial* victory over sin.[60]

Let's return again to the cross in this context. We can now see that evangelical universalists combine (a) the Arminian belief in a universal atonement with (b) the Calvinist belief in the efficacy of the atonement. This is not to suggest that the cross works salvation in people apart from a proper Spirit-enabled response to the gospel, only that salvation is a trinitarian project: the divine Father who sent his Son to die for sinners also sends his Spirit to work in them, sometimes over long stretches of time, leading them to the foot of the cross. And what is it that the cross effects? It makes peace, reconciling the world to God; it destroys sin; it defeats death and the hostile powers that stand against us. The universalist message is this: *Christ died for all out of God's love for all, and he did not die in vain.*

In an open letter to Dan Taylor (1738–1816), a well-known General (i.e., Arminian) Baptist, Winchester wrote,

> Did not Christ make a full and complete offering and propitiation for the sins of the whole world? It is [sic] not certain that his merits were far greater than the demerits of all mankind? Is he not the Lamb of God who taketh away the sin of the world? If Christ died for all men, without exception, as you grant, and removed all their iniquities, and bore them away, and reconciled all to God by his death while they were enemies: much more as he has paid so great a price for their ransom, he will recover them out of their lost estate, and save them by his life. . . .

60. *UR*, sec. 3, ans. 6.

I conclude, that let sin be ever so great, the grace of God is greater: and if you will have it that sin is of *infinite magnitude*, I hope you will not deny the propitiation of Jesus Christ, which he made for all sins, the same character. Therefore if you, magnify sin, and insist upon the greatness of its demerit, I will endeavor to magnify the all powerful Redeemer above it, and speak of his power to redeem all the human race, for whom he shed his blood.[61]

Biblicism

The gospel to which we must conform is testified to by scripture. Any universalism that claims to be evangelical has to maintain a "high view" of scripture.[62] This means that, for the evangelical universalist, the salvation of all people must be believed to be either a direct teaching of the biblical texts or inferable from the direct teachings of those texts. And it must be the teaching not only of a few select texts but of the Bible taken as a whole. This is precisely why my argument in *The Evangelical Universalist* eschewed proof-texting and sought to build on the entire span of scripture, from Genesis to Revelation.

An evangelical view of the Bible requires that some plausible account be given of scriptural texts that appear, at first blush, to teach the eternal damnation of some people. For the evangelical, such texts cannot simply be dismissed as the mistaken human ideas of their authors—not least because some of these teachings are those of Jesus himself! So the teachings of these texts must be able to be incorporated within the wider universalist vision. If they cannot, then the possibility of evangelical universalism should be abandoned.

61. Elhanan Winchester, *The Restitution of All Things Defended* (London, 1790), 35–36.
62. A certain degree of flexibility regarding what constitutes a "high view" of scripture must be allowed. Evangelicalism has always encompassed a certain variety, within limits, in the theology of scripture and the praxis of scripture reading. Inerrancy, for instance, while common, has never been an evangelical universal. Evangelical universalists fall on both sides of the inerrancy debate.

Evangelical universalists expressly assert their submission to the teaching of scripture. For Winchester, theology *was* biblical interpretation. As an evangelical, his oft-repeated conviction was that if the idea of the restitution of all things were unbiblical, it would *have to be* rejected. (And he often said that he would drop it instantly if any could convince him that it was not scriptural.) He even urged caution on the part of those considering it, calling them to weigh the biblical teachings very carefully before affirming Christian universalism. So the bulk of his work is an attempt to show that the diverse texts of the Bible are consistent with—and that, indeed, some positively teach—universal salvation. In this he was typical of all evangelical universalists. The same instinct was inscribed, for instance, into the Rule of Faith of the 1790 Philadelphia Convention of Universalists: "We believe the Scriptures of the Old and New Testaments to contain a revelation of the perfections and will of God, and the rule of faith and practice."[63] This was the very first article in the first attempt at a pan-universalist statement of faith, which surely says something about the evangelical roots of the movement.

As an illustration of later evangelical universalism, here, from the nineteenth century, is Andrew Jukes (1815–1901): "Believing, however, that the Holy Scripture, under God and His Spirit's teaching, is the final appeal in all controversies,—regarding it as the unexhausted mine from whence the unsearchable riches of Christ have yet still more to be dug out,—acknowledging no authority against its conclusions, and with the deepest conviction that one jot and one tittle shall in no wise pass from the law till all be fulfilled,—I turn to it on this as on every other point, to listen and bow to its decisions."[64]

63. "Rule of Faith, Philadelphia Convention of Universalists (1790)," sec. 1, "Of the Holy Scriptures," Unitarian Universalist Association, accessed March 8, 2023, https://www.uua.org/re/tapestry/adults/river/workshop7/175906.shtml.

64. Andrew Jukes, *The Second Death and the Restitution of All Things* (London: Longmans, Green, 1869), 17–18.

Of course, the great challenge for evangelical universalists is
that while they can point to texts that appear to assert universal
salvation, their opponents in the mainstream can likewise identify biblical passages that appear to assert that some people will
be forever damned. How is one to handle the Bible's two voices?

The heart of Winchester's hermeneutic is an attempt to find a
way of holding firmly to all the diverse teachings of the Bible—
not "in any wise to explain away or weaken, the force of either
the threatenings or promises, set forth in this wondrous book."[65]
The Bible speaks *both* of some in hell *and* of universal restoration; so, reasons Winchester, *both* those teachings must be true.
Therefore, any understanding of hell that excludes the promise
of universal salvation cannot be accepted. But Winchester was
well aware that this was the heart of the disagreement between
himself and more traditional Protestants. Those who took issue
with him felt that the hell texts were so clear that the promises
of universal salvation must be interpreted in the light of them.
Winchester, however, felt that the situation was exactly the reverse.
Everything hinges on which way one attempts to hold the biblical
teachings together.

Central to Winchester's case was what he took to be positive
promises of universal salvation.[66] For instance, Ephesians 1:9–10
pictures the goal of creation as the gathering together of "*all*
things" in Christ. Colossians 1:19–20 speaks of Christ reconciling "*all* things" that have been created to God, "making peace
through his blood, shed on the cross."[67] Revelation pictures "every

65. *UR*, sec. 4, ans. 14.

66. Winchester surveys these texts in various places. For example, *The Universal
Restoration* (1788); *An Attempt to Collect the Scripture Passages in Favour of the
Universal Restoration* (Providence, 1786); *A Letter to the Rev. C. E. De Coetlogon*
(London, 1789), 26–31.

67. Universalist readings of some texts are commonly accused of overinterpreting
the word "all." Winchester discusses at some length whether "all" literally means
"all" (*UR*, sec. 1, ans. 9). He argues that "all" means "all without exception" unless
the context indicates that it does not (e.g., 1 Cor. 15:27). He is, in my judgment,
correct.

creature in heaven and on earth and under the earth" worship-
ing the Father and the Son—the creating and redeeming God
(Rev. 5:13). And Romans 5:18–20 claims that all those who died
in Adam (i.e., every human being) will be made alive in Christ
and that grace will undo all the damage that sin has done. From
Philippians 2:9–11 and 1 Corinthians 12:3, Winchester proposed
a syllogism:

1. If all people (every tongue in creation) shall confess Jesus as
   Lord (Phil. 2:11), and
2. if no one can confess Jesus as Lord except by the Spirit
   (1 Cor. 12:3), then
3. the Spirit must work effectually in all people, leading them
   to confess Christ as Lord.[68]

Winchester took the confession mentioned in Philippians 2:11
to be salvific (and not one of forced subjugation) in light of the
OT text Paul used (Isa. 45), which has a clear global-salvation
context—"Turn to me and be saved, all you ends of the earth"
(v. 22)—and in light of general Pauline teaching on the link between confessing Jesus as Lord and salvation.[69] Critically, in terms
of his hermeneutic, Winchester wrote, "As endless damnation appears to me to be *against the promises*, I cannot hold to it as an
article of my faith; but were there no promises or intimations to
the contrary in Scripture, I should not require it to be threatened
in any stronger terms than it is. . . . My difficulty arises from these
express promises of God."[70]

This argument was a fundamental one in evangelical universalism, and even outside of it. For instance, the Anglican cleric
Thomas Allin (1838–1909) makes much of the idea that universalism allows one to hold together all that the Bible teaches in a

68. *UR*, sec. 1, ans. 7.
69. *UR*, sec. 1, ans. 7.
70. *UR*, sec. 1, ans. 7.

way that he believes nonuniversalism cannot. He too makes the case for reading the judgment texts in the light of the salvation texts.[71] Where Allin differs from Winchester is that he reinforces this hermeneutic with an extensive study of patristic teaching. Many of the early fathers, says Allin, interpreted the hell texts in light of God's wider redemptive scheme. We should follow their model.

Thomas Talbott has influentially argued that universalists are in exactly the same situation regarding biblical interpretation as all other evangelicals.[72] He invites us to consider the following three propositions:

1. All human sinners are equal objects of God's redemptive love in the sense that God, being no respecter of persons, sincerely wills or desires to reconcile each one of them to himself and thus to prepare each one of them for the bliss of union with him (Lam. 3:22, 31–33; Ezek. 33:11; 2 Cor. 5:19; 1 Tim. 2:4; 2 Pet. 3:9; 1 John 2:2).

2. Almighty God will triumph in the end and successfully reconcile to himself each person whose reconciliation he sincerely wills or desires (Job 42:2; Ps. 115:3; Isa. 46:10b, 11b; Rom. 5:18; 1 Cor. 15:27–28; Eph. 1:11; Col. 1:20).

3. Some human sinners will never be reconciled to God and will therefore remain separated from him forever (Matt. 25:46; Eph. 5:5; 2 Thess. 1:9).

Now, it is *impossible* to coherently affirm all three of these propositions. At least one of them *must* be false. Thus, Calvinists traditionally affirm 2 and 3 (but deny 1), and Arminians affirm 1 and 3 (but deny 2). Clearly, Calvinists and Arminians see 1 and 2 as

71. Thomas Allin, *Christ Triumphant: Universalism Asserted as the Hope of the Gospel on the Authority of Reason, the Fathers, and Holy Scripture*, annotated edition, ed. Robin A. Parry (Eugene, OR: Wipf & Stock, 2015), chaps. 8–9.
72. Talbott, *Inescapable Love of God*, 37–41.

evangelical-compatible beliefs, even though they themselves embrace only one of these two propositions. The universalist embraces 1 and 2—both evangelical-compatible beliefs, as we have seen—but is therefore compelled to deny 3. Furthermore, each of the three propositions enjoys biblical support—or so it seems at face value. (The verses he mentions as examples are noted above.) Talbott's point is that Calvinists, Arminians, and universalists are all in the same boat here. Whatever one's stance, unless one wishes to say that the Bible teaches contradictory things, one is compelled to interpret some texts in ways that differ from their prima facie meaning. The point is that this is not a special problem for the universalist—it is an issue for *all* evangelicals, whatever their theological position. Talbott proceeds to argue on various grounds that reinterpreting eschatological judgment texts (and rejecting proposition 3) is a theologically preferable route to the Calvinist or Arminian alternatives.

Andrew Jukes offers a theological explanation for why scripture seems to speak with two voices on the issue of universalism. Christ, he says, is the key to understanding the *nature* and *teaching* of scripture. The definitive divine self-revelation in the incarnation shows us that the invisible God is manifest *in* and *through* creation *to* creation. As such, the divine is revealed under a created veil.

> So exactly is Holy Scripture the Word of God; not half human and half divine, but thoroughly human, yet no less thoroughly divine, with all treasures of wisdom and knowledge revealed yet hidden in it. And just as He, the Incarnate Word, was born of a woman, out of the order of nature, without the operation of man, by the power of God's Spirit; so exactly has the Written Word come out of the human heart, not by the operation of the human understanding, that is the man in us, but by the power of the Spirit of God directly acting upon the heart, that is, the feminine part of our present fallen and divided human nature.[73]

73. Jukes, *Second Death*, 5–6.

How does this apply to the tensions in the Bible?

> Like Christ's flesh, and indeed like every other revelation which
> God has made of Himself, the letter of Scripture is a veil quite as
> much as a revelation, hiding while it reveals, and yet revealing while
> it hides; presenting to the eye something very different from that
> which is within . . . ; therefore, as seen by sense, it is and must be
> apparently inconsistent and self-contradictory. Both these points
> are important; for if God's revelations of Himself are veils, even
> while they are also manifestations; and if therefore they are and
> must be open to the charge of inconsistency and contradiction;
> this fact will help us to understand, not only why Scripture is what
> it is, but also how to interpret its varied truths and doctrines.[74]

As divine revelation veils as it reveals, *apparent* contradiction is
to be expected, and misunderstanding is an ever-present danger.
Indeed, scripture even *seems*, at times, to set forth "unworthy
and even untrue statements about God."[75] Why would God reveal
himself in such an ambiguous way? Jukes appeals to the classic
principle of divine accommodation: "The reason is that God is
love, and that in no other way could He ever have reached us where
we were, or brought us where He is. God therefore was willing to
seem inconsistent, and for a while to come into man's likeness,
to bring man back to His likeness. . . . Here is the reason for the
human form of the Divine Word in Scripture. Had that Word
come to us as it is in itself, we should no more have apprehended
or seen it than we see God."[76]

So the hermeneutical question is "not what this or that text,
taken by itself or in the letter, seems to say at first sight, but rather
what is the mind of God, and what the real meaning in His Word
of any apparent inconsistency."[77] The apparent inconsistency in

74. Jukes, *Second Death*, 9–10.
75. Jukes, *Second Death*, 13.
76. Jukes, *Second Death*, 14–15.
77. Jukes, *Second Death*, 18–19.

this case is between universal salvation texts and hell texts. What is the key? *The gospel.* The two sides of the tensions need to be maintained in a way that does justice to the good news. The problem with the traditional view of hell is that "in asserting one side of Scripture, it is obliged, not only to ignore and deny the other side, but to represent God in a character absolutely opposed to that in which the gospel exhibits Him."[78] The hermeneutical key, in Jukes's view, is a big-picture account of the story of creation and redemption in which all the parts find their places and in which even tricky texts (about election and judgment, say) are understood within a picture of global redemption. This he seeks to offer in his book.

One sees this high view of scripture, moreover, in the vast amount of space devoted by evangelical universalists to biblical exposition and in how they respond to biblical objections in their defenses of universal salvation. For instance, while severe postmortem judgment is fully incorporated within a universalist vision, *everlasting* judgment is trickier,[79] so great energy was expended in showing that scripture nowhere asserts *everlasting* damnation. Perhaps the topic that received the most discussion in this regard was the Greek word *aiōnios*—the adjective used to describe the eschatological punishment in Matthew 25:46 and 2 Thessalonians 1:9. Countless studies sought to demonstrate that it (and the Hebrew word *'ôlām*) should not be translated as "everlasting." Indeed, those who immerse themselves in the historical texts here can become weary of the seemingly everlasting discussions on *aiōnios*, but such studies do indicate the seriousness with which evangelical universalists felt compelled to take biblical texts.

---

78. Jukes, *Second Death*, 26.

79. We should note that Relly and Murray believed everlasting punishment was the just wage of sin, but they insisted that Christ had paid that price for all. To them, hell is everlasting punishment, but none go there. Most universalists, however, have seen postmortem suffering as corrective, educative, or purifying, with salvation as its ultimate goal. This is not to claim that "hell" saves (*only Christ saves*); rather, it is to affirm that "hell" can help expose the true nature of sin, stripping us of our self-delusions.

Conversionism

Evangelical universalism is also in harmony with the classic
evangelical emphasis on the importance of responding appropriately to the gospel call and of being born again. The widespread
misconception that if God will save everyone then it does not
matter how we live or whether we trust in God or walk in holiness is utterly misplaced. The gospel is about the salvation of the
world through Christ, restoring humanity as the divine image
bearer. *This does not happen apart from a free human response
to the divine initiative.* Sure, this free human response is impossible apart from divine enabling—it is a gifted response, but that
does not change the fact that evangelical universalists believe that
apart from our loving trust in and surrender to God there is *no*
participation in the salvation achieved in Christ. Converting to
God is essential.

This converting to God is a journey with a beginning (new
birth), a long middle (sanctification), and an ending (glorification). And each phase of this conversion journey involves right
Spirit-enabled human response to God. Those who think that
evangelical universalism makes conversion an optional extra have
simply failed to understand evangelical universalism.[80]

It is also worth noting the way that the initial evangelical conversion experience itself—the so-called "born again" experience—
was seen by some to contain the seeds of universalist thought.
Evangelical conversion had a very particular shape in the eighteenth century. One first experienced oneself as a dreadful sinner
in the sight of God, worthy of wrath, and unable to save oneself.
After a period of wrestling with this dreadful truth, the gospel
word broke through into one's heart as a word of great release,
and one abandoned oneself to Christ with joy and gratitude. This

---

80. On the criticism that the possibility of postmortem salvation undermines
the motivation for evangelism, see Heath Bradley, *Flames of Love: Hell and Universal Salvation* (Eugene, OR: Wipf & Stock, 2012), chap. 6; MacDonald, *Evangelical
Universalist*, 168–72.

was Winchester's own experience. In that moment of conversion he felt "the fullness, the sufficiency, and willingness of Christ to save me and all men. . . . And O how did I long, that every soul of Adam's race might come to know the love of God in Christ Jesus! And I thought I could not be willing to live any longer on earth, unless it might please God to make me useful to my fellow creatures."[81] This "experimental knowledge" many evangelicals found as an almost spontaneous aspect of their conversion. They *felt* that Christ can save all, and they earnestly desired that he do so. Do we, asked Winchester, have more compassion for creatures than God himself? Surely not! Do not these feelings come from the Holy Spirit and express God's own desires?[82]

Activism

Early Continental pietistic universalism arose in the midst of a fervent renewal movement (and in the case of the Moravians, a missional movement), and early British and American evangelical universalism arose at the radical edge of the Evangelical Revival, so it is unsurprising that in all these manifestations there were many highly motivated preachers. All the better-known names of the fledgling movement were preachers, many of them with demanding itinerant ministries—Petersen, de Benneville, Böhler, Relly, Rich, Streeter, Murray, Winchester, and others. Indeed, some of them pushed themselves to the very limits of their health in pursuit of their gospel-preaching ministries.[83]

Preaching of the gospel was also motivated, for some at least, by an evangelical fear of divine judgment. Winchester is yet again an interesting case study. He was a successful preacher who had led many people to Christ prior to and following his embrace of the universal restoration. Even as a universalist, Winchester took

81. *UR*, sec. 3, ans. 2.
82. *UR*, sec. 3, ans. 2.
83. I say that, not to recommend such a punishing approach to ministry, but simply to observe how activist and missional the early movement was.

the warnings of hell very seriously.[84] His evangelistic address to the youth of Philadelphia (1785) is telling in this regard. He pleaded earnestly with them to take the fate of their souls seriously in light of "the shortness of time, the uncertainty of life, the certainty of death and judgement, the worth of the soul, the duration of eternity, the torments of the damned, and the happiness of the righteous."[85] And thus he esteemed the task of the evangelist very highly. In a sermon commemorating the work of John Wesley, he says, "There is no business or labour to which men are called, so important, so arduous, so difficult, and that requires such wisdom to perform it [as that of the soul-winner]. The amazing worth of the soul, makes the labour so exceeding [sic] important, and of such infinite concern."[86] Given the conversionist stance of evangelical universalism, Winchester's words here are not hard to appreciate.

Evangelical activism has always included more than gospel preaching. Early evangelical universalists tended also to be concerned with issues of social and political equality. There was a natural extension from belief in God's redemptive love for all people to a belief in the equality of all people before God. After the 1830s, denominational Universalists became active opponents of slavery.[87] This opposition ran back to their evangelical roots, with later universalists appealing to the example of Elhanan Winchester,

84. Some objected that people would not take "hell" seriously if one could be redeemed from "hell." Winchester had little time for this, pointing out that if someone were to say, "Earthly punishment must come to an end, so I can see no difference between being made an heir to the king and being hanged, drawn, and quartered for high treason," we would think that person insane (UR, sec. 4, ans. 14). There was, however, a disagreement within the early movement—which developed into a full-blown split in the nineteenth century—between those, like Murray, who felt that there was no postmortem divine punishment for anyone to fear, for Christ had already paid the full penalty and God would not extract it twice, and those, like Winchester, who taught that there was a punishment to come and to fear.

85. Elhanan Winchester, An Address to the Youth of Both Sexes in Philadelphia (Philadelphia: Towne, 1785).

86. Elhanan Winchester, A Funeral Sermon for the Reverend Mr. John Wesley (London: Gillet, 1791), 3.

87. See Miller, Larger Hope, chap. 21.

himself an open critic of slavery. Winchester caused controversy in his South Carolina Baptist church by insisting on evangelizing enslaved people as well as white people, and in 1788 he published a fierce tirade against the slave trade (a sermon preached in 1774 in the colony of Virginia).[88]

On the issue of women's rights, various universalists took a stand. In the eighteenth century, John Murray's second wife, Judith Sargent Murray (1751–1820), was an unusually outspoken advocate of women's equality and rights. "Her views of gender relations represented the 'cutting edge' of what passed for feminism in eighteenth-century America."[89] In the nineteenth century, we find the Anglican evangelical Josephine Butler (1828–1906), who was involved in various women's rights campaigns, including ones that addressed women's education and issues relating to the welfare of prostitutes. Butler rarely spoke of her universalism, but she did embrace the larger hope.[90] Consider also Hannah Whitall Smith (1832–1911).[91] Smith was raised an American evangelical Quaker and was later influenced by the Brethren in the UK. She played a major role in the promotion of the holiness, or higher life, message in both America and Britain—indeed, she was an instigator of the Keswick movement.[92] Her preaching was widely

88. Elhanan Winchester, *The Reigning Abominations, especially the Slave Trade, Considered as Causes of Lamentations* (London: Trapp, 1788). On the controversy over evangelizing slaves, see Parry, "Baptist Universalist."

89. Sheila L. Skemp, *Judith Sargent Murray: A Brief Biography with Documents* (Boston: Bedford/St. Martin's, 1998), vii.

90. "Josephine felt that she had to reject the traditional concept of hell in part because she considered it forced God into the divine role of eternal oppressor. And though people may have committed heinous deeds, the omnipotence of God would overrule and his purpose of universal salvation *would* be fulfilled, for 'beneath the abyss of hell there is yet the bottomless abyss of the Love of God.'" Lisa S. Nolland, *A Victorian Christian Feminist: Josephine Butler, the Prostitutes and God* (Carlisle, UK: Paternoster, 2004), 251.

91. Interestingly, the original edition of Smith's autobiography contains a lot of universalist material, but the publishers removed it from subsequent editions. Hannah W. Smith, *The Unselfishness of God and How I Discovered It* (London: Nisbet, 1903).

92. The Broadland conferences, starting in 1874 and leading to the initiation of the Keswick movement, were a response to interest generated by Smith's

influential, and her books on holiness sold millions of copies.
She too was an advocate of women's suffrage and women's rights
in higher education. In addition, she helped found the Women's
Christian Temperance Union (temperance being another issue
that universalists campaigned on).

The early American universalists were a notoriously individualistic bunch, deeply suspicious of ecclesial authority and
resistant to any perceived infringements on their freedom. However, they were strong advocates of toleration, having so often
experienced discrimination themselves. Politically, most of them
were great believers in the American republican aspiration. For
instance, John Murray, although a recent immigrant from Britain,
believed in the American experiment and served as a chaplain in
Washington's Continental Army in 1775, until ill health forbade
it. Indeed, Washington himself came to his defense when other
chaplains complained about having a universalist serve as chaplain. Winchester, too, a fifth-generation American, was a great
enthusiast for the revolution, composing a political catechism for
use in American schools (1796) and a dreadful book of patriotic
hymns (1776). One of Winchester's friends and fellow universalists was the physician, writer, and humanitarian Benjamin Rush
(1745–1813), one of the signatories of the Declaration of Indepen-
dence. Rush saw universalism as inherently connected with the an-
timonarchist stance of Christian republicanism. "The American
Revolution was, in Rush's mind, but one step in the working
out of the divine millennial plan for the new nation about to be
born. Universalism was to be a major vehicle for establishing both
political and religious equality under the aegis of a benevolent

---

universalism. Hannah and her husband chaired the meetings. Other Christian
universalists—George MacDonald and Andrew Jukes—also played a key role. Furthermore, the theology of the universalist Thomas Erskine was influential at Broad-
lands through the presence of Emilia Gurney and Julia Wedgwood (Darwin's niece),
both great admirers of his work. The Keswick movement continues to this day as
a conservative evangelical gathering, largely oblivious to the role that universalism
played in its roots.

deity."[93] It was, for Rush, the faith that best complemented the new American republic. As he put it in 1791, "A belief in God's universal love to all his creatures . . . is a *polar* truth. It leads to truth on all subjects, but especially upon the subject of government. It establishes the *equality* of mankind."[94]

All of this is simply to point out that the belief that God was in Christ reconciling the world to himself does not lead to inertia. That "all shall be well" does not mean that all *is now* well—that we can sit back while the world goes to hell. Holiness matters. Justice matters. Mission matters. God invites his church to participate in the ministry of reconciliation, inviting creation to be reconciled to God. This makes activism a natural orientation.

The Diversity of Evangelical Universalism

By now it should be clear that evangelical universalism has always been a diverse phenomenon, as has evangelicalism itself. There is agreement that all will (or hopefully will) be redeemed through Christ's atoning work, but there is also considerable disagreement. Obviously there is disagreement about matters that don't directly relate to matters of total salvation. For instance, some universalists have a "spiritualist" view of the sacraments, considering them as symbols of inner realities that believers are not required to practice in a literal, outward sense; others have a Zwinglian view, considering them as symbolic acts pointing us to Jesus's past redemptive work; and still others have very high sacramental and pneumatic views, according to which baptism and the Eucharist are a spiritual means of grace through which Christ is present and working by his Spirit. Evangelical universalists share the same range of

---

93. Miller, *Larger Hope*, 39. I hasten to add that while there is a "natural" connection, there is no *necessary* connection between universalism and republicanism. (God save the King!)

94. Benjamin Rush, *Letters*, ed. L. H. Butterfield, 2 vols. (Princeton: Princeton University Press, 1951), 1:583–84.

views on church government as evangelicals more broadly. And the same could be said on debated matters like the millennium, divine eternity, just war theory, and so on. However, there is also diversity in some areas of theology that do relate more directly to the question of universal salvation. In what follows, I shall simply mark out some of this diversity. It is not my intention to suggest that all the views presented are equally plausible.

Divine justice. The issue of hell is very much tied up with the issue of divine justice. Some see God's justice as primarily retributive: we get what we deserve. Others see it as primarily corrective or restorative. Yet others seek a middle ground, trying to incorporate aspects of both retribution and restoration.

Divine wrath and punishment. Related to the question of justice is the matter of God's fury and punishment. Some think God's wrath is primarily God's active punishment of sinners, while others see it as God's handing sinners over to the inherent consequences of their freely chosen sin. When we ascribe fury to God, are we making a claim about how God actually *feels* about sin and how he reacts to it, or are we speaking anthropomorphically? Are we speaking in terms of *how things seem to us* when God allows us to experience the consequences of our actions (it feels like God is punishing us in his anger)?[95]

The cross. All evangelical universalists see the cross as central to God's salvific work, but there is no common understanding of how it functions. Some embrace the classic evangelical penal substitution model of the atonement. Indeed, it was precisely James Relly's unwavering commitment to this model that led him to universalism![96] Many more, however, wish either to decenter (and

95. This debate long predates modern disquiet about divine violence and finds its origins in patristic deliberations on how best to make sense of biblical references to divine wrath. The differences between evangelical universalists mirror earlier differences between the church fathers.

96. It has long been argued within certain Calvinist circles that penal substitution + universal atonement = universal salvation. Because Calvinists rejected universal salvation, logic required that they limit the scope of atonement.

perhaps also reconfigure) penal substitution, placing it alongside other complementary models, or to reject it completely in favor of alternative understandings of the cross.[97]

Postmortem punishment. Most evangelical universalists, like patristic universalists, believe that there is eschatological judgment and punishment for all those outside of Christ. What makes them universalists is that they believe salvation is still extended to those who remain unsaved in the age to come—one can be saved by Christ from "hell"—and, eventually, all will accept this offer of salvation. However, there has always been a minority report, especially from some in the Reformed tradition, that disapproves of this way of setting things up. For instance, Relly claimed that because God has already punished the sin of all people once and for all in Christ, he cannot punish it again in hell.[98]

Hopeful and confident universalism. If we expand the scope of evangelical universalism beyond those I call "confident universalists" to include those who are open to the real possibility that all will be saved, and who hope and pray for it with cautious expectation, then a good few more folks fall into the evangelical universalist category (e.g., Alvin Plantinga and Rob Bell). Such hopeful universalists may draw back from "confident universalism" for a number of different reasons. For some, hopeful universalism is simply a halfway house on an ongoing journey between views. For others, the biblical evidence is too indeterminate for a confident affirmation of universal salvation. For yet others, hopeful universalism is a principled theological stance: we cannot, either because of divine or human freedom, be in a position to declare

97. Penal substitution was the default in early evangelical universalism. That changed in denominational Universalism with the publication of Hosea Ballou's hugely influential book *A Treatise on Atonement* (Randolph, VT: Sereno Wright, 1805). Ballou strongly repudiated such models.

98. This issue became a major conflict within denominational Universalism in the 1820s and 30s, between the "Ultra-Universalists," like Hosea Ballou and Thomas Whittemore, who claimed that divine punishment was experienced only in this life, and the "Restorationists," who argued for postmortem punishment.

either that all will or that all will not be saved. Such folks may reject the label "universalist," perhaps with some ferocity, but some still refer to them as hopeful universalists. Here we could include P. T. Forsyth, Karl Barth, and Thomas F. Torrance.

Inclusivism and exclusivism. Evangelical universalists can fall on either side of the inclusivism/exclusivism debate. Both sides agree that eternal life is found only in and through Christ, but they disagree about whether *explicit* knowledge of and faith in Christ is essential. Could, for instance, someone who had never heard of Jesus be saved through Christ if they responded appropriately to the revelation that was available to them? The issue was not really up for discussion before the twentieth century. Exclusivism seemed to be the default for universalists and nonuniversalists alike, though there were exceptions on both sides (e.g., Sadhu Sundar Singh and John Wesley). In more recent decades, inclusivism has made inroads into evangelicalism more broadly, and it is no surprise to find some universalists from evangelical backgrounds also drawn to the view.

Calvinist versus Arminian. Universalists can have differing opinions on the intersection of divine sovereignty and human freedom. Some may have very strong views of providence, seeing God as determining every event that occurs: We are free to the extent that God allows us to do what we choose to do, but even this freedom is compatible with divine determinism operating at a higher level. Everything that we freely choose to do, even sin, is determined by God in his grand purposes. Obviously, what makes such a Calvinist approach universalist is the additional affirmation that God will eventually cause all people to freely embrace the gospel. Arminian universalists, or those in that orbit, believe that human freedom is not compatible with divine determinism and that humans really can resist God, at least to an extent. This means that much that happens is not exactly as God wants it. However, God is able, in his wisdom, to engage us all in such a way that we will eventually choose to submit to Christ. (This is not the place to explore the extensive and sophisticated discussions of the relationship between freedom and universalism.[99])

Election. Related to the previous discussion, different universalists handle the biblical notion of election in different ways. For some, the notion is simply extended to include all humanity. Others see the elect as those chosen to believe the gospel in this life. Still others interpret election in terms of God's plan of salvation, which involves certain groups and individuals being chosen by God to serve specific purposes in God's global mission. They are elect, not instead of, but *on behalf of* the nonelect. Finally, some make a Barthian move and see Christ as the Elect One and all those who are united to Christ as *chosen in Christ* (Eph. 1:4), rather than as chosen to be in Christ, and as participating in his election for the sake of the world.[100]

The salvation of Satan. Here evangelical universalists can take one of several different routes. At one end of the spectrum, some restrict salvation to humanity and exclude fallen angels. At the other end, some affirm the eventual salvation of Satan and his demonic hordes. However, the latter may prefer to put it this way: Satan *as Satan* cannot be saved. The sinful self (Satan) must be damned for the new self (Lucifer) to be born, much as Darth Vader had to die for Anakin Skywalker to be redeemed. Between these extremes are those who remain agnostic on the extension of salvation beyond humanity and those who deny that Satan and the demonic forces have a positive ontological status. On the latter view, Satan is not a person but a mythic way of picturing the very real evil at work in the world, an evil that supervenes on complex human reality, both individual and social. When it comes to the devil, he is real, but *he is not a person.* Thus, the healing

99. On these discussions, see esp. Talbott, *Inescapable Love of God*, chap. 11; Kronen and Reitan, *God's Final Victory*.

100. For my own views regarding biblical teaching on election, see MacDonald, *Evangelical Universalist*, 222–42; and Robin A. Parry, "Universal Election: A Sketch," in *T&T Clark Handbook of Election*, edited by Edwin Chr. van Driel (London: Bloomsbury T&T Clark, 2023).

of creation will, by definition, annihilate Satan and his demonic forces, just as a wound ceases to exist when healing comes.

Interpreting specific texts. There is diversity in how particular "key" texts are interpreted. For instance, there is a range of different universalist attempts to make sense of the parable of the rich man and Lazarus, with its uncrossable chasm (Luke 16:19–31), or the parable of the sheep and the goats, with the "eternal" punishment of the goats (Matt. 25:31–46).

Handling tensions in the biblical text. How are we to do justice to the theological diversity in scripture, and how are we to discern unity in this diversity? Regarding hell, how are we to hold together texts that speak of global salvation and texts that speak of eschatological destruction? The majority evangelical approach has been to harmonize them. For traditional evangelicals, this means harmonizing them so as to exclude universalism; for evangelical universalists, it means harmonizing them so as to exclude everlasting hell. The danger here is of failing to do justice to the diversity of scripture. There is a growing minority report within evangelicalism that would prefer to find some way of maintaining a tension between the texts, of resisting what they see as an imposed theological coherence. Here a range of possibilities may open up for alternative evangelical universalist ways of handling hell texts, but as yet these have not been very much explored.

————————

I would like to conclude with a quotation from the closing paragraph of *The Evangelical Universalist*:

> Let me ask you to hold in your mind traditional Christian visions of the future, in which many, perhaps the majority of humanity, are excluded from salvation forever. Alongside that, hold the universalist vision, in which God achieves his loving purpose of redeeming the whole creation. Which vision has the strongest view of divine love? Which story has the most powerful narrative of

God's victory over evil? Which picture lifts the atoning efficacy
of the cross of Christ to the greatest heights? Which perspective
best emphasizes the triumph of grace over sin? Which view most
inspires worship and love of God, bringing him honor and glory?
Which has the most satisfactory understanding of divine wrath?
Which narrative inspires hope in the human spirit? To my mind
the answer to all these questions is clear, and that is why I am a
Christian universalist.[101]

101. MacDonald, *Evangelical Universalist*, 176–77. My thanks to Heath Bradley
and Alex Smith for comments on a previous draft of this chapter.

3

Post-Barthian Universalism

Tom Greggs

To speak of Karl Barth (1886–1968) as a "universalist" requires a heavy emphasis on the scare quotes that surround this description of his theology. As Barth himself once said regarding universal salvation, "I did not teach it, but I did not not teach it."[1] The question of whether Barth himself was some form of universalist is a hotly debated one within Barth studies. Barth did not consider himself a subscriber to *apokatastasis*, but it is clear nevertheless that Barth's work tends in a direction that has led many to consider him a universalist theologian—one whose theology suggests that no final limit can be placed on the love and grace of God in Jesus Christ. Indeed, there are various suggestive one-liners that seem to indicate that this description of Barth might be true, along with Barth's affirmation of Hans Urs von Balthasar's statement

1. Eberhard Jüngel, *Barth-Studien* (Zurich: Benziger, 1982), 51, my trans.

in a letter to his son, Christoph: "The dogma is that Hell exists, not that people are in it."[2] As he stated later in his life, the real danger for theology is to place too great a limit on the scope of salvation and the power of the gospel for all people.[3]

Although some have been at pains to point out in as strong terms as possible that Barth was not a universalist[4] (presumably because this issue has bearing on the ways in which Barth can be appropriated by and for orthodox, or neoorthodox, theology[5]), it is clear that aspects of Barth's theology suggest a hope in the ultimate salvation of all people. Barth's overt rejection of a dogmatic universalism[6] has not stopped other theologians from utilizing his work to advocate for a particular form of universal salvation, one that employs the deep insights that Barth's theology offers. Indeed, Barth has figured as something of a touchstone in ongoing debates about universal salvation, especially in English-speaking Protestantism.

In this chapter, the issue under discussion is not whether Barth was himself a universalist.[7] Rather, the issue to be considered is

2. Eberhard Busch, *Karl Barth: His Life from Letters and Autobiographical Texts* (London: SCM, 1976), 362.

3. Karl Barth, "The Humanity of God," in *God, Grace and Gospel*, Scottish Journal of Theology Occasional Papers No. 8 (Edinburgh: Oliver and Boyd, 1959), 50.

4. See Joseph D. Bettis, "Is Karl Barth a Universalist?," *Scottish Journal of Theology* 20, no. 4 (1967): 423–36.

5. This quest rests at the very heart of Barth interpretation. For those who would claim Barth as a neoorthodox theologian, the idea that he was some form of universalist is anathema. But in my judgment, the neoorthodox Barth does not do justice to the radicality and the modern nature of Barth's thought. On Barth and neoorthodoxy, see Bruce McCormack, *Orthodox and Modern: Studies in the Theology of Karl Barth* (Grand Rapids: Baker Academic, 2008).

6. E.g., Karl Barth, *Church Dogmatics*, ed. G. W. Bromiley and T. F. Torrance, 4 vols. (London: T&T Clark, 2004), II/2, 417: "If we are to respect the freedom of divine grace, we cannot venture the statement that it must and will finally be co-incident with the world of man as such (as in the doctrine of the so-called *apokatastasis*). No such right or necessity can legitimately be adduced." Hereafter this work is cited as *CD*. References to the German text of *Die kirchliche Dogmatik* will be cited as *KD*.

7. There is clearly a tension here—the tension of the one who "didn't teach" universalism but also "didn't *not* teach" universalism. The approach of identifying

how theology that understands itself as in some ways indebted to Barth might articulate a particular form of universalism following from some of the insights of his work. The question is, What particular form of universalism might arise from Barth's theology? Although Barth himself stops short of a thoroughgoing universalism, his theology potentially points to the logical conclusion that universal salvation is the end point of his thought. After all, Barth's ultimate silence about the issue is a silence preceded by a large amount of material that in its tenor and its logic offers what seems to be a crescendo of ultimate hope for the salvation of all people—a crescendo that others have heard, described, and sought to join.

Universalism (and most especially Barth's "universalism") is a topic on which I have already spilled much ink.[8] In the account I offer here, I wish to spend more time discussing more directly than I have previously the material that leads commentators to consider Barth a universalist—particularly, his account of the election of humanity in the life, death, and resurrection of Jesus Christ—and, more notably, *how* this material can shape an account of universalism. Rather than the question of whether Barth himself was a universalist, I want to pursue the question of what

---

and pointing to this tension as the hermeneutical key for understanding Barth's approach to the topic of universalism is a wise one, and there is much worth in presenting Barth's position on universalism as "reverent agnosticism" and "holy silence" (George Hunsinger, *How to Read Karl Barth: The Shape of His Theology* [New York, Oxford University Press, 1993], 134; George Hunsinger, *Disruptive Grace: Studies in the Theology of Karl Barth* [Grand Rapids: Eerdmans, 2000], 243). Barth's stopping short of stating that he is a universalist is, in the end, because of the object of theology for him and because of his own theological method in light of the object of theology. This point has been made extremely well by David W. Congdon in *"Apokatastasis* and Apostolicity: A Response to Oliver Crisp on the Question of Barth's Universalism," *Scottish Journal of Theology* 67, no. 4 (2014): 464–80.

8. See, e.g., my "'Jesus Is Victor': Passing the Impasse of Barth on Universalism," *Scottish Journal of Theology* 60, no. 2 (2007): 196–212; *Barth, Origen, and Universal Salvation: Restoring Particularity* (Oxford: Oxford University Press, 2009); "Pessimistic Universalism: Rethinking the Wider Hope with Bonhoeffer and Barth," *Modern Theology* 26, no. 4 (2010): 495–510; and *Theology against Religion: Constructive Dialogues with Bonhoeffer and Barth* (London: T&T Clark, 2011), chap. 5.

Barth can offer constructively for a contemporary articulation of universal salvation. To this end, this chapter first seeks to outline the shape of Barth's account of election and to uncover what it might offer for those who seek constructively to develop some kind of account of universal salvation. This account is one that we might term *particularist universalism*. The deeply particularist approach of Barth in relation to the election, life, death, and resurrection of Jesus Christ cannot be forgotten in any account of the scope of salvation that draws from his work, and therefore in any discussion of universal salvation that seeks to draw from his insights.

To emphasize this point further, the second section of this chapter aims to show that any account of universalism wishing to draw from Barth's logic cannot overreach its conclusions. The deep particularism of Barth's theology is such that the subject of theological reflection needs always to be remembered—Jesus Christ as the Revelation of God. The subject matter for any account of universalism following Barth should be Jesus Christ and Christ's victory over sin and death, not some principle of grace and its triumph in a dogmatic and principled account of universal salvation. The personhood and particularity of Jesus Christ provides a limit on the dogmatic claim to universalism, and if Barth's theology is used as the basis for an account of universal salvation, the "universalism" that follows from it should be one that is very much contained in scare quotes. Not a dogmatic principle, this kind of universalism should take the form of a hope grounded in Jesus, who is the Victor. To consider this theme, this section discusses one of Barth's major direct considerations of the question of universalism—his response to Berkouwer's book *The Triumph of Grace*—and from this draws constructive conclusions for universalist accounts.

The final section of this chapter continues with the theme of particularism in relation to universal salvation, looking at attendant themes that need to be considered in a theology indebted to

Barth: sin and unbelief, conversion, and the work of the Spirit in the lives of believers. It is intended that through this account a version of universalism that is deeply particularist can be offered— one that takes seriously the particularity of Jesus Christ and his life, death, and resurrection; the seriousness of sin and evil; the reality of reprobation and judgment; and the call to faith. Any theology that seeks to stand in some kind of relationship with Barth's thought and yet to move in a universalist direction cannot fail to do this.

Election and the "Logics" of Universalism

The primary dogmatic location those who draw upon Barth for an account of universal salvation look to is his radical redescription of the doctrine of election, a redescription that arose from Barth's refining and extending a theological insight gained from Pierre Maury's paper "Election and Faith" at the 1936 *Congrès international de théologie calviniste* in Geneva.[9] In understanding the subject and object of double predestination as Jesus Christ,[10] Barth considers the election of humans as that which takes place only in Christ; this effectively forms what might be called a "metaphysics of salvation," and this metaphysics of salvation describes a reality that encompasses all humanity in its scope and effect. Describing universalism after Barth requires attending to the major themes in relation to salvation that his account of the eternal election of Jesus brings to the fore. A degree of detailed exegesis of Barth's theology is required here. However, this exegesis will bring out the essential Christocentric particularism that is key to understanding any form of universalism that seeks to be in dialogue with Barth.

9. *CD* II/2, 154–55, 191–94.
10. The christological account of election is a move that we can already see beginning in a very early form in Barth's 1924–25 lectures at Göttingen. See Karl Barth, *The Göttingen Dogmatics* (Grand Rapids: Eerdmans, 1991), 468, 470. However, the simultaneity of Christ as elected *and* electing comes only after 1936.

A Radical Movement from the Tradition

The first thing to be said here is that there needs to be in this account an honest recognition of Barth's significant shift away from the inherited, classic Protestant Reformed tradition regarding election. If this kind of universalism rests on Barth's radical redescription of election, it is of paramount importance to understand what Barth is doing in this redescription, and how this differs from other accounts of election, as well as from the majority inherited tradition of classical Western theology.

While Barth retains the logics of double predestination, his account of election marks an enormous movement away from Calvin's theology (and, through Calvin, from Augustine) in that one group is no longer identified as the saved and another as the damned, but Jesus Christ himself is identified as the one who eternally elects divine rejection in order that those who deserve rejection (because of sin) might be elect.

This is in stark contrast to Calvin's understanding of double predestination. Calvin famously writes, "We say that God once established by his eternal and unchangeable plan those whom he long before determined once and for all to receive into salvation, and those whom, on the other hand, he would devote to destruction. We assert with respect to the elect, this plan was founded upon his freely given mercy, without regard to human worth; but by his just and irreprehensible but incomprehensible judgment he has barred the door of life to those whom he has given over to damnation."[11] According to Calvin, some are ordained to eternal life and others to eternal death; this is individualized in relation to each person such that each individual is either elected or rejected, predestined to life or to death.[12]

Double predestination is the antithesis of universal salvation. Election marks the efficient cause of human salvation, with the

11. John Calvin, *Institutes of the Christian Religion* (Louisville: Westminster John Knox, 1960), 3.21.7.
12. Calvin, *Institutes*, 3.21.5.

material cause being the mediatorial office of Christ. This mediatorial office and work of Christ arises, for Calvin, because of God's eternal plan,[13] thereby determining that the decree to elect precedes the decree to appoint Christ to his mediatorial office. But in this office, Christ "in common with the Father" claims for himself the right to choose (some), and as such makes himself the "Author of election."[14] There is, therefore, in Calvin, a Christocentric component to election, but this is preceded by the decree to elect some and reject others.[15]

Barth follows Calvin's linkage of election and the work of Christ but pushes further the Christocentric component, and he questions whether Calvin in the end demands a "hidden God" behind God's revelation in Jesus Christ: "Is it the case . . . that in the divine election as such we have to do ultimately, not with a divine decision made in Jesus Christ, but with one which is independent of Jesus Christ and only executed by Him?"[16] Instead, for Barth, straightforwardly, "As we have to do with Jesus Christ, we have to do with the electing God."[17] Jesus Christ is, therefore, not only the elected human but also the divine Elector, and this gives material content to the act of election.

The Election of Jesus Christ

Barth's account of election is a new one, and it radically realigns the manner in which he speaks of predestination and the resultant destiny of humanity to salvation or perdition. If it is true that double predestination is the antithesis of universalism, to see Barth's account of election as the basis on which one might begin to describe some form of universal salvation might seem very odd.

13. Calvin, *Institutes*, 2.12.4.
14. Calvin, *Institutes*, 3.32.7.
15. Cf. *CD* II/2, 149–50. Barth attends to the fact that, for the older orthodox, there is a distinction between two works of God—first, the work of predestination and, second, an encounter with Jesus Christ.
16. *CD* II/2, 64.
17. *CD* II/2, 54.

However, rejecting the classical binarized notion of predestination as concerning one portion of humanity elected to eternal salvation and another elected to eternal damnation, Barth instead speaks of election in terms of the one and single election of Jesus Christ. It is this rejection of election as pertaining to two portions of humanity that has vast implications for any account of universalism following after Barth. The focus of election is not the saved and the damned, as classes of human beings, but Jesus Christ—who is himself the eternal subject and object of divine election. It is not the Christian, or the church person, or the church community that is elect; Jesus Christ alone is the elected human being, and the others are elected *in him*. Barth puts the matter thus:

> Before all created reality, before all being and becoming in time, before time itself, in the pre-temporal eternity of God, the eternal divine decision as such has as its object and content the existence of this one created being, the man Jesus of Nazareth, and the work of this man in His life and death, His humiliation and exaltation, His obedience and merit. It tells us further that in and with the existence of this man the eternal divine decision has as its object and content the execution of the divine covenant with man, the salvation of all men.[18]

The eternal willing of God to be God in Jesus Christ (in the concrete form of his birth, life, death, and resurrection) is the divine eternal decision (from the very beginning, in eternity itself) to be the God who is in covenant with humanity, who is *for* humanity, and who brings about "the salvation of all."[19]

In the ordering of decrees, there is no priority of the election of some to salvation and others to damnation before the decision

18. *CD* II/2, 116.
19. Barth even considers Judas Iscariot at length (*CD* II/2, 458–506). See the discussion of Barth's treatment of Judas in David F. Ford, *Barth and God's Story: Biblical Narrative and the Theological Method of Karl Barth in the "Church Dogmatics"* (Bern: Peter Lang, 1985), 85–93.

for and of the Son of God to become incarnate in time. The election of humanity (*in toto*) exists only in the prior election of Jesus Christ. It is only *en autō* (in him) that humans are elected. The power of this "in" is significant. Being "in Christ" should not be understood instrumentally, such that election is by virtue of Christ and his work. On this, Barth is emphatic: "Nor does ['in Him'] mean only through Him, by means of that which He as elected man can be and do for them. 'In Him' means in His person, in His will, in His own divine choice, in the very basic decision of God which He fulfils over against every man."[20] Humanity is elected in Jesus Christ's own humanity. His election is the unique election of the electing God who elects Godself, but as such this election includes all humanity that is elected in Christ: "His election is the original and all-inclusive election; the election which is absolutely unique, but which in this uniqueness is universally meaningful and efficacious, because it is the election of Him who Himself elects."[21]

This act of election is gracious, as it is a free act of the grace of God, who wills to be for another. There is nothing in and of humanity itself (even the humanity of the human Jesus) that determines that there is any requirement or need of election. There is "indeed no merit, no prior and self-sufficient goodness, which can precede His election to divine sonship."[22] Nothing can compel the election of God; it is an act of sheer and superabundant grace. But this sheer grace is a grace that incorporates all humans who are elected in God's eternal election of humanity in Jesus Christ as the beginning of all of God's ways. Election is something God accomplishes in his decision in Jesus Christ, and as such it is an act of sovereign grace. This glorious, loving election (involving God's condescension, patience, freedom, and overflowing) is not something God is bound or compelled to do;

20. *CD* II/2, 117.
21. *CD* II/2, 117.
22. *CD* II/2, 118.

it is a free outworking of the free covenant of grace.[23] This grace, to be gracious, is free and divine. To see it as sheer grace, indeed, one needs to see its freedom in God.[24] A universalism after Barth has to draw upon the sheer grace of God as expressed in the singular and particular human being Jesus Christ. This is the first and last thing to say about election.

From a universalist perspective, it is impossible to separate the love of God and the will of God. Salvation is not plan B to a failed plan A. The salvation, therefore, that comes from election, although it happens in time in the concrete life of the incarnate Jesus, is not a second act of God that follows creation and the fall. It is the primary act of God. God is the God of election—the God who determines Godself to be the God of salvation. There is no God behind God's willing to be the God of grace and salvation, the God who is for humanity, the God who is God in Jesus Christ. As Barth puts it, "In Himself, in the primal and basic decision in which He wills to be and actually is God, in the mystery of what takes place from and to all eternity within Himself, within His triune being, God is none other than the One who in His Son or Word elects Himself, and in and with Himself, elects His people. In so far as God not only is love, but loves, in the act of love which determines His whole being God elects."[25] The election of Jesus Christ in God's gracious self-giving is the eternal willing of God. Put starkly, in Barth's words, "In the beginning with God was this One, Jesus Christ. And that is predestination."[26] This bespeaks not only the economy of the divine life but the nature of God.

In starting with Jesus Christ, this doctrine of election determines that Christian speech about God is less a philosophical

23. CD II/2, 9–11.
24. CD II/2, 19–20. Indeed, Barth says we cannot enter the council of God, as God made this decision.
25. CD II/2, 76.
26. CD II/2,145.

reflection on various themes about the nature of monotheism and more a Christian understanding of the God of election—the God revealed to humanity in the person of Jesus Christ.[27] However, in stating this, universalist accounts after Barth must not make such kataphatic claims as to imagine that they have grasped the deep mysteries of God. This claim does not remove the mystery of God or divine otherness. It cannot be so self-assured as to fail to see the *positive* mystery of the divine life. Instead, describing God in relation to the eternal election of Jesus Christ gives content to the very meaning of mystery within Christian theology. This mystery now is that of God and of humanity being caught up in the eternal will of God, and as such it is a mystery of "incomprehensible light" rather than a mystery that is suggestive of ignorance or darkness.[28] This mystery points to the majesty of a God who is known to us as revealed in Jesus Christ, rather than to the majesty of a God who is "not known to us."[29] In Jesus Christ, humanity can know who the electing God is. The God of election is not a God who might as well damn humans as save them, or with whom there can be any sense of arbitrariness. Rather, God is altogether the God of the gospel—the God who is revealed to us in the grace of Jesus Christ.[30]

The Election of Reprobation

But what does this mean in relation to God's righteousness, or in relation to the judgment and holiness of God? Does this emphasis on the gracious election of God remove the need to

27. CD II/2, 148.
28. CD II/2, 146.
29. CD II/2, 146.
30. Barth rejects the idea of a *decretum absolutum* and replaces it with Jesus Christ: "This decree is Jesus Christ, and for this very reason it cannot be a *decretum absolutum*." However, even in so doing, Barth does not believe this rationalizes or simplifies the mystery of the divine life. To put Jesus Christ in the place of the *decretum absolutum* is still mystery—the mystery in which "our life is hid with Christ in God" (CD II/2, 158).

speak seriously of judgment and the reprobate state? It is here that the truly radical contribution of Barth's theology to those after him who seek to offer an account of universalism comes to the fore: Jesus's election is an election to assume the *negative* side of predestination on humanity's behalf—to suffer the rejection humanity deserves on account of human fallenness. There is no longer a need to understand the potential of universal salvation as removing the seriousness of reprobation. It is not a question of mercy *or* judgment in the divine life and economy, as both mercy *and* judgment are incorporated in the election of Jesus Christ.

Any theology that tends in a universalist direction should not fail to acknowledge the judgment of God, the seriousness of sin, and the fallen condition of human beings. Election is not only an act of kindness and condescension; it is also a self-giving,[31] as it is an election to suffer and to die,[32] to bear the judgment that humans in their sin should bear. God foresaw this need for human judgment from all eternity.[33] But for and from all eternity, God also elected Christ as the first of God's ways, as the one who would have the power to overcome the temptation by which, in Adam, humanity fell. His overcoming of temptation overcomes the temptation of all who are elected in him (all the descendants of Adam). For all eternity, God elects this obedient One, Jesus Christ, who is obedient for humanity, and in whose obedience all humanity is elected.[34]

This is potentially the most radical economic aspect of Barth's complete redescription of election. God elects, in Jesus Christ, to bear the rejection that humanity, in its rejection of God, deserves. God elects, in Jesus Christ, to allow God's judgment on humanity (for its rejection of God) to be borne by his Son. God elects to

31. CD II/2, 121.
32. CD II/2, 122. Barth prepares the exegetical ground for this in CD II/2, 116–18, 122.
33. CD II/2, 122.
34. CD II/2, 123.

take reprobation unto Godself as its rightful execution and as that act which makes even judgment grace for us. Barth writes, "This checking and defeating of Satan must consist in His allowing the righteousness of God to proceed against Himself instead of them. For this reason, He is the Lamb slain before the foundation of the world. For this reason, the *crucified* Jesus is the 'image of the invisible God.'"[35]

Election is, for all eternity, the electing of God to be Jesus Christ and to bear the rejection humanity deserves because of human iniquity. Any account of universalism that takes Barth's theology seriously has to give a thoroughgoing account of the economy of God as expressed in the cross of Christ. It is the very particularity of Jesus's life, death, and resurrection that is the basis and content of election. Barth references Revelation 13:8 here, pointing to Jesus as the one slain even before creation, and he states that this cruciform life is the image of the invisible God, since this is the eternal image of the divine life of the second person of the Trinity. Jesus, as the Son of God, takes the wrath of God upon himself so that it does not fall on those "in Him."[36] God accomplishes this because "from all eternity He loves and elects us in His Son, because from all eternity He sees us in His Son as sinners to whom He is gracious."[37]

Because of the obedience of the Son, however, the mercy of God remains faithful to Jesus, as he was ready (by bearing the rejection of God for those "in Him") to fulfill the will of God. There is a steadfastness in both the Father and the incarnate Son, and it is this that sees Satan resisted, defied, and defeated. This divine steadfastness that defeats Satan is "the resurrection of Jesus from the dead, His exaltation, His session at the right hand of the Father."[38]

35. CD II/2, 123.
36. CD II/2, 124.
37. CD II/2, 124–25.
38. CD II/2, 125.

These acts of divine grace are, however, based in the eternal identity of the divine life, not in the election of one group or in the response of the believer. And this is key for those who wish to draw on this idea in developing an account of universal salvation. God's eternal identity is to be the One who determines Godself from all eternity to be "for humanity." It is not in a second act of God but in the very first decree that it is possible to see that grace is the eternal identity of the divine life—as, in election, the divine life is ordered toward the whole of humanity (not merely toward one group of humans) as the sinners to whom God is gracious.[39]

Universalism after Barth has to describe itself fully in relation to the salvation of human beings by grace as a result of the eternal willing of the divine life to be for creatures in the life, death, and resurrection of the Son of God.[40] It is this Christocentric particularism that is the key to understanding the universal salvific purposes of God. The eternal willing of God takes shape in the historical form of Jesus Christ's life and death as God wills to give Godself to fallen humanity.[41] This is a costly act of divine grace. In the fellowship that exists in the covenant God establishes between Godself and humanity, God is set to lose and humanity to gain. Here is the unpacked form of double predestination, an

39. Barth engages in a long discussion on supra- and infralapsarianism (*CD* II/2, 127–45). He refines the position of supralapsarianism and states, "God does not will and affirm evil and the fall and an act of sin on the part of this man. . . . But for the sake of the fullness of His glory, for the sake of the completeness of His covenant with man, for the sake of the perfection of His love, He wills and affirms this man as sinful man" (*CD* II/2, 141). According to Barth, God does not will and elect *homo labilis* for the fall but, rather, for the "uplifting and restitution by an act of divine power; the demonstration in time, in the creaturely sphere, of His eternal self-differentiation" (*CD* II/2, 142).

40. *CD* II/2, 161. I have been criticized with regard to my earlier work that I did not attend sufficiently to the cross. Although such criticism failed to see the particular purpose of the work on Barth and Origen (attending to the economic logics of Spirit and Son in salvation), the same criticism could not be leveled against the work offered here, as attention to the cross is central to the case I am making.

41. *CD* II/2, 161–62.

account with potential for universalist theology that does not ne-
glect the negative side of election. As Barth states, "If the teachers
of predestination were right when they spoke always of duality, of
election and reprobation, of predestination to salvation or perdition, to life or death, then we may say already that in the election
of Jesus Christ which is the eternal will of God, God has ascribed
to man the former, election, salvation and life; and to Himself He
has ascribed the latter, reprobation, perdition and death."[42]

A post-Barthian universalism is not one that proceeds out of
optimism regarding the innate goodness of humanity—out of a
sense that humanity will, given time and experience, will itself
toward the divine life. This account is one in which the true drama
of salvation is addressed; in which the Son of God faces the risk
and threat; in which humanity's fall jeopardizes the honor of God;
in which human sinfulness stands at the frontier of that which is
impossible, excluded from and contradictory to the will of God;
and in which—crucially—God's election is grace and love in that
God elects God's own suffering for us in Jesus Christ on the cross.[43]
The historic form of this is seen in the narrative of the Gospels:
in Jesus Christ, God elects Judas as an apostle, even though he
will betray Jesus; the sentence of Pilate as a revelation of God's
judgment on the world; Golgotha as God's kingly throne; and the
tomb and garden as the scene of resurrection.[44]

This is how God loves the world. This is the manner in which
God elects the negative part of predestination. Chiastically, God
elects for Godself the rejection humans deserve so that the rejection of humanity could be taken up into the electing will of God
for humanity. Barth writes, "In so far, then, as predestination
does contain a No, it is not a No spoken against man. In so far
as it involves exclusion and rejection, it is not the exclusion and
rejection of man. In so far as it is directed at perdition and death,

42. *CD* II/2, 162–63.
43. *CD* II/2, 163–64.
44. *CD* II/2, 165.

it is not directed to the perdition and death of man."[45] This rejection is what humanity deserves. God did not have to act in such a way as to forgive; but God freely binds Godself to humanity such that God takes to Godself the torment and punishment humans deserve. In this, God does not overlook (or negate the significance of) human sinfulness, but God wills to expiate this human sinfulness through God's mediating work in Jesus Christ on behalf of humanity in its state of rejection.[46] Humanity needs the justification that comes to it in Christ. But Barth is clear that this justification is eternal and cannot be reversed: "Rejection cannot again become the portion or affair of man."[47] There is no condemnation for those who are "in Christ"—that is, those whom God eternally determines Godself to be for, namely, humanity.[48] This account of election, if it is to be used in service of a universalist account of salvation, makes plain that such an account has to address both the mercy *and the justice* of God, as expressed in the radical account of the electing will of God; and, more powerfully still, that the divine identity of Christ is such that *God* takes reprobation unto Godself as its rightful execution and as that act which makes even judgment grace *for humanity*.

Christocentric Particularist Universalism

The positive consequence of this account of the election of Jesus Christ for humanity, however, is that in electing *the entire race of humanity in Jesus Christ*, God leaves no room remaining for the shadow side of election for humanity—damnation or rejection. Indeed, in placing the doctrine of election in its particular Christocentric form within the doctrine of God, and in offering content to the divine decision to elect and reject such that there is no God who might as well save or condemn humans behind

45. CD II/2, 166.
46. CD II/2, 166–67.
47. CD II/2, 167.
48. CD II/2, 167.

the decision to be incarnate in time, the only logical conclusion one is left with, economically, would seem to be that salvation is universal: election is the sum and whole of the gospel *in nuce*. But this universal effect is founded in the very particularity of God's singular act in Jesus Christ. God's economy as Creator, Reconciler, and Redeemer is grounded in the very particular, eternal decision of God's grace, in the divine decision to be for humanity.[49] Election is always with the goal of sending the eternal Son,[50] who will bear on the cross the rejection humanity deserves for the sake of humans receiving reconciliation and redemption. In the eternal Son, God shows that God is for Jesus, and that in Jesus God is for the entire human race.[51]

This particularism does not rest only in the singular act of God in Jesus Christ but also in the existence of those with the *form* of the "elected" or "rejected" in the world following the life, death, and resurrection of Jesus Christ. This facilitates further accounts of universalism in the way it accounts theologically for those who reject or ignore the message of God's salvific will. The particularism and significance of the life of faith or of the rejection of the gospel remains key. Here, again, Barth's theology has considerable potential to aid an account of universalism: there is a theological account of those within the world who appear to be either elect or reprobate. By Barth's account, even those who seem to have the form of the "rejected" have the purpose of manifesting the grace of the gospel,[52] just as those who have the form of the "elected" have the purpose of witnessing directly to the election of humanity in Jesus Christ. This is a potential universalism that makes sense of the two seeming conditions of humanity. The role that exists for the "rejected" is to move from being reluctant, indirect witnesses to becoming direct witnesses to the election of Jesus Christ and

49. *CD* II/2, 14.
50. *CD* II/2, 25.
51. *CD* II/2, 25.
52. *CD* II/2, 457.

his community.[53] That we, as creatures, could reject our election
might be an impossible possibility; nevertheless, there is nothing
that can change God's decree *for* humanity. Here it is worth quoting Barth at length:

> If we truly hear, then in face of this election and its meaning it is
> not possible for us not to be able to hear or obey that Yes, not to
> will to be amongst those who are affirmed by God. This is not a
> possibility but an impossibility. It is a turning of the sense of that
> election into nonsense. It is a descent into the abyss of the divine
> non-willing and the divine non-electing. Even in such a descent
> the creature cannot escape God. Even in this abyss it is still in the
> hands of God, the object of His decision. Yet that does not mean
> that it has been flung, or even allowed to fall, into the abyss by God
> Himself. God is and God remains the One who has decided for
> the creature and not against it. It is by love itself that the creature
> is confounded. Even there, in the midst of hell, when it thinks of
> God and His election it can think only of the love and grace of
> God. The resolve and power of our opposition cannot put any
> limit to the power and resolve of God. Even in our opposition
> there comes upon us that which God has foreordained for us. But
> that means that what comes upon us cannot alter in the slightest
> the nature and character of the foreordination which is God's
> decree. In that decree as such we find only the decree of His love.
> In the proclaiming and teaching of His election we can hear only
> the proclaiming of the Gospel.[54]

The creature can be "in the midst of hell" and "in this abyss," but
nevertheless the creature's resolve and power (to reject its election)
"cannot put any limit to the power and resolve of God." Both
the present condition and the ultimate reality can be accounted
for here. Condemnation is the shadow side of the impossible

53. CD II/2, 458. Barth works this out in a long, detailed footnote about Judas
(see CD II/2, 458–506).

54. CD II/2, 27.

possibility of the rejection by humans of divine grace: it is, we might say, a possible impossibility.

This is closely related to a key concern that must be raised in relation to any universalist account of salvation—the concern that God remains free and sovereign. God has the freedom to reject the creature and condemn it, but in grace, there is always a divine "Nevertheless" toward the creature. God executes God's freedom not in allowing the creature to perish freely but in rescuing the creature from the destruction that the creature has fallen into. God chooses Yes and not No because No is the attitude of the creature and God's election in grace is Yes. There is nothing, for Barth, that will inevitably shatter the love of God. That God elects in the way God does is God's freedom *not from the creature but for the creature.* Universalism need not be spoken of such that it removes divine freedom and sovereignty. If one follows Barth's logic, universalism can be spoken of such that it underscores God's freedom and sovereignty. In God's sovereignty, the creature cannot escape God's grace. Instead, the creature must fulfill the divine will even in the creature's condemnation—a point that is "confirmed in the Nevertheless with which [God] rescues the creature from condemnation and ordains it to blessedness, notwithstanding the decision of the creature, in opposition to it, in reversal of that mistaken decision, in the reconstitution of it by His own prior decision."[55] Humans cannot push their freedom over and above God's freedom. To state that the responsive nature of human engagement with God's election of humanity flouts divine righteousness is a nonargument. Righteousness means that God maintains God's own order, by which standard all other order is disorder. In this, the righteousness of God helps the creature to see outside the election of God by looking into the abyss and yet being led back to God's election. God's righteous order is God's opposition to the creature, but it is an opposition that exists *in*

55. CD II/2, 29.

loving-kindness. Divine righteousness is God's forgiving (rather than avenging) sin. We cannot distinguish God's righteousness from God's mercy, but universalism need not mean that either is flouted by the human rejection in time of the gift of God's salvation in Christ.[56]

Nor need universalism fail to account for the existence of the community of faith and the importance of the decision of faith. The election of the community and individuals (who are elect only for the sake of the community[57]) comes to belong to the sphere of the simultaneous divine-human self-election in Christ. Human election occurs only in Christ's prior election and cannot be abstractly separated from this. Included in Christ's election is the election of the other—the many "whom the electing God meets on this way."[58] This is no abstract account of election that does not have concrete effects for individuals and communities. The church has a purpose, which is to proclaim, "In Jesus Christ, thou, too, art not rejected—for He has borne thy rejection—but elected."[59] We may say, therefore, that election and rejection belong together in the primal decision of Christ to self-elect the rejection belonging to humanity. Nothing can flout this eternal electing will of God. Jesus Christ elects humanity as electing God, "electing them in His own humanity."[60]

56. *CD* II/2, 33–34.
57. See *CD* II/2, 196: "It is not men as private persons in the singular or plural. It is these men as a fellowship elected by God in Jesus Christ and determined for all eternity for a particular service." For Barth, the "other" involved in election is designated as community. This community covers both Israel and the Church, as one sees *CD* II/2, §34 (it is important to note that this paragraph comes before §35, "The Election of the Individual"). In *The Theology of Karl Barth* (San Francisco: Ignatius Press, 1992), Hans Urs von Balthasar correctly asserts that it is for the sake of the community that the individual is chosen. He sees the initiative of Barth in placing the community as a middle term between Christ and the individual as one of an outward opening: "It breaks open the narrowly individualistic coloring that the Church's claim to be the means of salvation now possesses and opens her to the world" (183). The Church becomes, therefore, "an *open* space" (183).
58. *CD* II/2, 195.
59. *CD* II/2, 322.
60. *CD* II/2, 117.

An account of universalism that draws on Barth's theology will always be a universalism that is radically particularist in its presentation: it will be a universalism that has its internal logics in relation to the singular act of God in Jesus Christ. Jesus's election is unique, but in its uniqueness it is the original and all-inclusive election of all humanity. Drawing on such logic, Barth insists, "Reconciliation is a comprehensive occurrence, embracing many in the One in whom it was made, and through the many embracing all. . . . In Him the world is converted to God. In Him man is the friend of God and not His enemy. In Him the covenant which God has faithfully kept and man has broken is renewed and restored."[61] And elsewhere: "The case of all men is advocated and conducted by this One, all men being included in this One in the covenant as it is perfectly maintained and restored on both sides. There is no one, therefore, who does not participate in Him in this turning to God. There is no one who is not himself engaged in this turning. There is no one who is not raised and exalted with Him to true humanity. 'Jesus lives, and I with Him.'"[62] The particularity of Jesus Christ and his work has universal significance for humanity: Jesus Christ embraces all human living and dying in his own very particular life, death, and resurrection.

An account of universal salvation that articulates itself in relation to the being of humanity in Christ (or participatory union with Christ)[63] need not exist at the expense of more forensic language to describe the atonement. It is not simply in the *decision* to be elect but in the *historical event* of the crucifixion and resurrection of Jesus that atonement is fulfilled.[64] Even this more forensic

61. *CD* IV/1, 251.
62. *CD* IV/2, 271.
63. On participation in Christ, see Adam Neder, *Participation in Christ: An Entry into Karl Barth's "Church Dogmatics"* (Louisville: Westminster John Knox, 2009).
64. On this, see my essay, "The Order and Movement of Eternity: Karl Barth on the Eternity of God and Creaturely Time," in *Eternal God, Eternal Life: Theological Investigations into the Concept of Immortality*, ed. Philip Ziegler (London: T&T Clark, 2016), 1–24.

account can have a scope that is potentially universal if one reads the substitutionary work as taking place for and including *all* humanity. So, for example, Barth states,

> Because the God against whom the man of sin contends has judged this man, and therefore myself as this man, in the self-offering and death of Jesus Christ His own Son, putting him to death, and destroying him; and because He has revealed and continually reveals him as this one who is judged and put to death and destroyed in the resurrection of Jesus Christ from the dead and His being and living and speaking and witness for all ages. Because the verdict passed in His resurrection from the dead unmasks this old man, showing what every man is before God, and therefore what I myself am before Him, the man who is judged and put to death and destroyed. All this came upon Jesus Christ *for every one of us and therefore for me*, in our place and therefore in my place.[65]

The execution of the decision of God in time does not stand in contradiction to the eternal decision to elect but is the historical content of the decision. There is a soteriological objectivism in Barth's account precisely because Barth's soteriology is consistent with his account of election: God's decision to bear rejection in Christ results in the cross, and it is therefore through the cross that humanity finds itself reconciled to God. As George Hunsinger puts it, "Jesus Christ is the inclusive human being in a sense that is universal and universally valid. . . . The 'ontological connection' that establishes our being in Christ pertains not just to believers, but to all other human beings and to every human being as such."[66] This is true as much for forensic language as for participatory language.

The purpose of this section has been to outline the particular logical form that Barth's work takes in relation to his account

---

65. *CD* IV/1, 390–91, emphasis added.
66. Hunsinger, *How to Read Karl Barth*, 128–29.

of election, which has led some to draw upon his theology as a significant resource for contemporary accounts of universalism. However, a further significant theme that any account of universalism drawing from Barth must address is the nondogmatic (in the sense of nonabsolutized or nonprincipled) form that Barth insisted any statement regarding the ultimate scope of God's salvation in Christ must take. This form arises from addressing the subject of election—Jesus Christ, rather than any principle of grace. It is to this that we now turn.

Getting the Subject Matter Straight: Jesus Christ, Not a Principle of Universal Grace

Barth engaged in direct discussion of the potential universalist implications of his redescription of election. This material provides not only assistance with understanding Barth's own position on universal salvation but also (and more significantly for this chapter) material content for contemporary discussions of universalism. Here, Barth's great contribution to the discussion of universalism has been to draw the direct discussion away from any dogmatic implication or principle of universal salvation, so as to order and refocus the question back directly to Jesus Christ and to Christ's victory. Any account of universalism after Barth is wise to attend to this. It is the victory of Jesus Christ (and not universalism) that is the most appropriate direct subject matter of any account of the scope of salvation. The role of theology in this area is to point to the victory of Jesus Christ without turning this into some kind of universal principle. Universalism should not express itself as such; it should simply describe, indicate, and account for the life, death, and resurrection of Jesus Christ, and the victory over sin, death, and hell achieved in and by him. This is the ultimate statement a Christian can make. It is here that an account that tends in a universalist direction must end in terms of the force of its claims.

Rejecting the Charge of Universalism

The mistake of drawing out the conclusion dogmatically can be seen in G. C. Berkouwer's *The Triumph of Grace in the Theology of Karl Barth*. The title of Berkouwer's book comes from a phrase Barth deploys in *Church Dogmatics* II/2: "This history [of Jesus Christ's election] is a triumph only for God's grace and therefore for God's sovereignty."[67] Berkouwer considers this theme the hermeneutical key to unlocking Barth's redescription of election. He sees Barth affirming, from a pastoral motivation,[68] that to believe we humans are rejected by God at any point is "the perverse belief in what God has not decreed."[69] According to Berkouwer, Barth's account of election is overwhelming gospel:

> Barth is certainly concerned about the *light* and the *certainty* and the *triumph* of grace. The darkness and the rejection have a distinct place in his treatment of election, but as darkness and rejection whose removal was negotiated for us at Golgotha, that is to say, they are treated as borne by Jesus Christ. To put it differently, the rejection of man has a place in Barth's doctrine of predestination only in the sense that it is carried, put away and destroyed, by Christ. In this sense, *double* predestination lies at the heart of Barth's doctrine. For him election does not mean the irresistibility and the triumph of an almighty "sovereignty." It means the triumph of *grace*.[70]

While Berkouwer attends to Barth's overt rejection of *apokatastasis*, he nevertheless concludes that this rejection sits uneasily and illogically with the structural argument of the account of election Barth offers. Berkouwer states, "There is no alternative to concluding that Barth's refusal to accept the apokatastasis cannot

67. *CD* II/2, 194; cf. *KD* II/2, 214.
68. G. C. Berkouwer, *The Triumph of Grace in the Theology of Karl Barth* (London: Paternoster, 1956), 95.
69. Berkouwer, *Triumph of Grace*, 107.
70. Berkouwer, *Triumph of Grace*, 107.

be harmonized with the fundamental structure of his doctrine of election."[71] Others have followed suit in their critiques of Barth's account of election, claiming that the only logical implication there can be to Barth's account of election is universalism. The most recent repristination of Berkouwer's argument comes from Oliver Crisp: "To quote Schopenhauer's dictum, an argument is not like a cab. You cannot pay off an argument when you have gone as far as you want."[72] One way to respond to this logic is by pointing out the numerous occasions Barth denied universalism outright. So, for example, in his discussion of the election of the individual, Barth writes,

> It is [God's] concern what is to be the final extent of the circle. If we are to respect the freedom of divine grace, we cannot venture the statement that it must and will finally be coincident with the world of man as such (as in the doctrine of the so-called apokatastasis). No such right or necessity can legitimately be deduced. Just as the gracious God does not need to elect or call any single man, so He

71. Berkouwer, *Triumph of Grace*, 116.

72. Oliver D. Crisp, "The Letter and the Spirit of Barth's Doctrine of Election: A Response to Michael O'Neil," *Evangelical Quarterly* 79 (2007): 64. For various different versions of Crisp's argument, see Oliver D. Crisp, "On Barth's Denial of Universalism," *Themelios* 29 (2003): 18–29; Oliver D. Crisp, "'I Do Teach It, But I Also Do Not Teach It': The Universalism of Karl Barth," in *"All Shall Be Well": Explorations in Universalism and Christian Theology, from Origen to Moltmann*, ed. Gregory MacDonald (Eugene, OR: Cascade Books, 2011); Oliver D. Crisp, "Barth and Jonathan Edwards on Reprobation (and Hell)," in *Engaging with Barth: Contemporary Evangelical Critiques*, ed. David Gibson and Daniel Strange (New York: T&T Clark, 2008).

An excellent response to Crisp's general approach is found in Congdon, "Apokatastasis and Apostolicity." This piece makes claims that are accurate about Barth's theological approach as a whole. As my own work indicates, my concern is simply Barth's universalism more narrowly. Congdon points out that my approach does not go far enough. I would contend, rather, that we are seeking to answer different questions. Congdon claims that Barth's primary concern is to describe not the objective and general operations of God in the world but, instead, "the existential determination and subjective participation of the one called to bear witness to Jesus Christ" (464). As this chapter points out, however, the existential determination and subjective participation of the Christian involve faithful witness to the constant and objective work of God in election and reconciliation.

does not need to elect or call all mankind. His election and calling do not give rise to any historical metaphysics, but only to the necessity of attesting them on the ground that they have taken place in Jesus Christ and His community. But, again, in grateful recognition of the grace of the divine freedom we cannot venture the opposite statement that there cannot and will not be this final opening up and enlargement of the circle of election and calling. Neither as the election of Jesus Christ, the election of His community, nor the election of the individual do we know the divine election of grace as anything other than a decision of His loving-kindness. We would be developing an opposing historical metaphysics if we were to try to attribute any limits—and therefore an end of these frontier crossings—to the loving-kindness of God. We avoid both these statements, for they are both abstract and therefore cannot be any part of the message of Christ, but only formal conclusions without any actual substance.[73]

Here, it seems clear that Barth is rejecting full-blown universalism. That is, Barth rejects overtly what Berkouwer and his followers see as the only possible outcome of the logical implications of Barth's own work—specifically, the logical direction of Barth's account of election (which I outlined above). However, critics of Barth (old and new) argue that this kind of rejection of the implications of Barth's theology by Barth is illogical and self-contradictory.

Some defenders of Barth's "orthodoxy" point to his actualism, as in John Colwell's account: "In the authentic temporality which is God's eternity the faith, hope and love of individual men and women are genuinely comprehended within the event of election."[74] Others suggest that for Barth divine freedom is such that it makes the salvation of all (Christian or non-Christian) uncertain. Hence,

73. CD II/2, 417–18.

74. John Colwell, "The Contemporaneity of the Divine Decision: Reflections on Barth's Denial of 'Universalism,'" in Universalism and the Doctrine of Hell, ed. Nigel M. de S. Camerson (Carlisle, UK: Paternoster, 1991), 158.

Joseph Bettis: "Barth does not reject universalism because the future of the pagan is uncertain. He rejects universalism because the future of all men is uncertain. Rather than ask whether Barth attributes too much to Christ's work, the question is whether Barth attributes enough to Christ's work."[75] However, such views seem a long way from the tenor of Barth's own emphatic sense that election is *good* news, and they seem out of step with his movement away from the idea of a God who might as easily condemn and reject a human as elect and save her. It may seem, in light of the kinds of accounts that Bettis and Colwell offer, that Barth stands in some kind of equidistant point between limited atonement and universalism, and certainly in *Church Dogmatics* IV/3, §70.3 ("The Condemnation of Man"), Barth seems to come closest to the idea that humans can ultimately refuse their election. But even in this direct discussion, the leaning ultimately is almost always toward a universal scope for salvation.[76] Indeed, it is difficult to deny that the tendency and direction of Barth's theology, and especially its tone, is hopeful for the salvation of all humanity. It seems that those who point away from this simply do not represent the general optimism about the ultimate fate of humanity that is present throughout Barth's theology.[77]

What are we to make of this, then? How do we reconcile the logical implications of Barth's reworking of election with the denial of overt universalism that is also present in his writing? How do we understand the comfort brought in the election of Jesus Christ in relation to Barth's concern not to fall into a metaphysical universalism? Is there a kind of universalism on offer here, or is Barth's denial so strong that any theology that draws on his work must simply reject any possibility of universalism and offer

75. Bettis, "Is Karl Barth a Universalist?," 433.
76. E.g., *CD* IV/3, 478.
77. See David Fergusson, "Will the Love of God Finally Triumph?," in *Nothing Greater, Nothing Better: Theological Essays on the Love of God*, ed. Kevin J. Vanhoozer (Grand Rapids: Eerdmans, 2001), 195.

a correction to readings that tend in this direction? Here it is wise
to attend specially to what Barth himself said about the critique of
universalism and about universalism's potential for contemporary
theology.

Not Universalism but the Victory of Jesus

Barth's own engagement with the question of universalism in
relation to Berkouwer makes it clear that the questions just posed
speak in ways that evince a failure to see the true subject matter
that theology should describe. This is a major contribution to the
question of universal salvation for contemporary theology: clarifying what its true object should be. Barth considered Berkouwer
correct in his analysis of the implication of Barth's theology for
universalism and did not respond to this issue with the level of
anxiety that many of Barth's commentators have regarding the
seeming universal scope of the soteriological implications of his
work. Barth offers a critique of Berkouwer's work in paragraph
69 of "The Glory of the Mediator," under subparagraph 3 (his description of "Jesus Is Victor"). But *at no point does Barth limit the
scope of salvation or question the extent of salvation* described
in Berkouwer's account. He dedicates a long small-font section
to Berkouwer's description of his work,[78] and in this section he
speaks of "the respect which it [*The Triumph of Grace*] deserves"
and observes that "Berkouwer has undoubtedly laid his finger on
an important point."[79] Barth's concern, instead of being about
the scope of salvation directly, revolves around the book's title,
which seems to indicate that Barth understands Christianity as
an absolutely "triumphant affair."[80] Despite the propensity for
polemic that Barth had, and the extent of the critique of Barth's

78. CD IV/3, 173–80. I have discussed this section in detail previously. The following paragraphs are rewritten versions of ideas published in my "Jesus Is Victor,"
used with permission.
79. CD IV/3, 173.
80. CD IV/3, 173.

work that is present in *The Triumph of Grace*, Berkouwer is prin-
cipally criticized for the title he gives his work: "If I am in a sense
understood by its [*The Triumph of Grace*'s] clever and faithful
author, yet in the last resort cannot think that I am genuinely
understood for all his care and honesty, this is connected with the
fact that he tries to understand me under this title."[81]

This title, Barth feels, should be replaced with the title of the
subsection under which he writes: "Jesus Is Victor." It is important in this discussion to attend carefully to what criticisms Barth
levels at Berkouwer, and equally important to attend to *what he is
not dismissing* in his very positive initial assessment of the book.
With regard to the latter, it is interesting to observe that Barth
never overtly rejects (nor does he mention) universalism per se;
this is not, it seems, the fear that Barth has. What he rejects are
some of the *implications* that Berkouwer draws from this con-
ceptualization of divine grace, not the extent of the positively
objective soteriology itself. Barth does not remove or even reduce
the emphatically positive ultimate message of the eternal election
of Jesus Christ, but he clarifies the sense in which this is to be
understood—most determinately *in Jesus Christ*. The account
draws out even further the form and depth of the particularism
discussed thus far. A theology that tends in a universalist direction should recognize its object: Jesus Christ, and the believer's
existential participation and determination in Christ. This means
that the dogmatic claim to universalism is not one a Christian
should make. This is explained by Barth in four points that draw
emphatic attention to themes present in his account of election.

First, theology cannot proceed on the basis of a christological "principle."[82] Not even election can take priority over Jesus

81. *CD* IV/3, 173.
82. Sauter is no doubt correct when, regarding a different issue, he writes, "When
Barth uses the word 'principle,' it connotes nothing less than the theological equiva-
lent of a major industrial accident, if not a nuclear power plant explosion which
can no longer be contained within tolerable limits." Gerhardt Sauter, "Why Is Karl

Christ, because "we are not dealing with a Christ-principle, but with Jesus Christ Himself as attested by Holy Scripture."[83] By making Christ a principle, Berkouwer has wrongly understood Christ primarily to be the "mighty executive organ of the divine will of grace,"[84] giving *truly* christological thinking only a secondary place. This undermines the appropriate methodological approach for addressing election, whose subject matter should be Jesus Christ. One cannot use even grace as a principle: election concerns Jesus Christ as the one who is elector and elected, and the one who as such bears the rejection due humanity. Humanity is elected in a person and not in a principle, and thus the *Gnadenwahl* (gracious election) cannot be understood as foundational or primary. Instead, grace must be understood through the person of Christ.

Second, in Jesus one deals with a *free* person and his free act, such that Jesus Christ cannot simply be grasped "in the sense of conceptual apprehension or control."[85] Jesus is not an abstract principle engaged in a battle with evil *in abstracto*; Jesus is a living person. Yet, this Jesus is a person in whom one cannot have limited confidence. As Johann Christoph Blumhardt asserts, the superiority of Christ to his opponent can end only in Christ's triumph. This is decided from the very commencement because "the One who is the First will also be the Last."[86] However, this reality is not such that it can lead to Jesus being replaced with the "principle" of the triumph of grace or the principled universalism that flows from it.

Third, election does not deny the reality of evil.[87] The charge that all history is sewn up in universalist-leaning accounts and that

Barth's *Church Dogmatics* Not a 'Theology of Hope'? Some Observations on Barth's Understanding of Eschatology," *Scottish Journal of Theology* 5 (1999): 407–29.

83. CD IV/3, 174.
84. CD IV/3, 175.
85. CD IV/3, 176.
86. CD IV/3, 176.
87. CD IV/3, 177.

they deny evil its reality are undermined by the double predestination of the life of Christ. Only under the motif "Jesus is Victor" can one understand the nature and reality of evil. Evil has a reality as "Nothingness" (*das Nichtige*).[88] In speaking of "nothingness," Barth speaks of something that does not exist as God or God's creatures do; nothingness has no basis for its being. This is not to deny nothingness the existence to which it has no right. Evil has reality in the existence we give it. But to speak of the victory of Jesus is to see nothingness in relation to Christ and his work, and thus in its ultimate "absolute inferiority."[89]

Fourth, stemming from all of this, speaking of Jesus and his victory emphasizes the historical encounter between God and evil that cannot be sublated by some universalist principle.[90] In understanding God's relationship to evil, it is clear that "*from the very outset*" God is infinitely greater and stronger than evil. However, one is not to understand this statement as a principle that dissolves history. God's encounter with the world is seen in the narrative of the life of Jesus. Rather than removing any sense of history, it is only *in the history of Jesus* that humanity can know God and evil, and the relationship of each to the other. In narrating the life of Christ, one sees that there is no "easy 'triumph of grace,'"[91] of the sort that might be found in a dogmatic, principled universalism. The victory of Christ involves triumph over evil through the cross, not a metaphysical principle to which God is somehow bound. Moreover, this is a history and a conflict in which humanity must engage in Christ: "Only victory is to be expected in view of its commencement, in view of Jesus, who has already fought the battle. Yet we have this confidence only with the last and bitter seriousness enjoined and demanded by this commencement by Jesus. Neither hesitant qualifications nor

88. See *CD* III/3, §50, "God and Nothingness."
89. *CD* IV/3, 178.
90. *CD* IV/3, 179.
91. *CD* IV/3, 179.

rash and slothful assurance are possible at this point."[92] Jesus
Christ's victory should be the subject of the hope of humanity
in God's salvation—not a principle of universalism that might
suggest the particularity of Jesus's life and the contemporary
struggle against sin and evil are unnecessary.

Not Limiting the Gospel but Recognizing the Particularity of Christ and the Believer in Him

As we see from this engagement, it is not the task of the theologian to reject the final victory of Christ (Barth never limits the
scope of salvation in response to Berkouwer) but to reject a particular (and wrong) understanding of the *means* by which this
victory is achieved—namely, an understanding that avoids the
particularities of the life, death, and resurrection of Jesus Christ.
Rather, salvation is offered to humanity in its election *in* Christ—
the Christ of whom it must be said, "Jesus is Victor." It is in the
history and narrative of the life, death, and resurrection of the
incarnate Christ that our election takes place in him. If theology is
going to tend in a universalist direction, then rather than focus on
the dogmatic principle of universalism, the theologian should attend to the reality that the election of humanity in Christ means an
election in a life, in a person—in the one who lived, was crucified,
and was raised. When Barth offers his overt statements rejecting
universalism, therefore, we might suggest he is claiming that there
is always a need for doctrine to attend to the particularity of the
person of Jesus Christ in his concrete life and the particularity of
the subjective implication of this life for the lives of believers—
particularities that cannot be gained from a principle.[93]

Since election is the election of a *person*, it is the determination of a person. Therefore, the question arises of the human self-

---

92. *CD* IV/3, 180. It is from this that Barth moves into his discussion of the drama and
war and history of the reconciliation into which humanity is drawn (*CD* IV/3, 181ff.).
93. See Congdon, "*Apokatastasis* and Apostolicity."

determination that corresponds to *this* determination. Election in
the *person* of Jesus allows space, in Christ's own free humanity,
for the subsistence of human freedom in a way that a principle
never can. John Webster's discussion of the ethical implications
of *enhypostasis* is instructive on this point.[94] In Webster's words,
because election is in the person of Jesus Christ, "human reality,
and therefore human agency, are *'enhypostatically* real,' drawing
their substance from the human reality of Jesus Christ."[95] This is
not to merge the two realities, but to recognize that our humanity
exists from and in his. Indeed, Barth overtly addresses the charge
of Christomonism: "It does not mean that Jesus Christ has merged
into world-occurrence and world-occurrence into Him, so that we
can no longer speak of them as separate things. This would be
Christomonism in the base sense of that unlovely term. What it
does mean is that according to the true insight of the people of
God the twofold form of world history loses the appearance of
autonomy and finality, the character of an irreconcilable contradiction and antithesis, which it always seems to have at a first glance."[96]
World-occurrence and the history of humanity still continue after
the incarnation of Jesus Christ,[97] but the contradiction and antithesis is *ultimately* removed. It is not that reality is dissolved into a
greater reality but, rather, that the very reality of the particularity
of the person of Jesus provides the basis for the existence of the
"twofold form of world history," and in that way for the very reality
of all particularity. Barth's pointing toward the statement "Jesus is
Victor," rather than toward a principle of grace, allows room for

94. John Webster, *Barth's Moral Theology: Human Action in Barth's Thought*
(Edinburgh: T&T Clark, 1998), 88ff. Although *enhypostasis* is not a doctrine Barth
uses overtly in his discussion of election, it is used clearly in Barth's thought both
before and after the doctrine of election. On *an-* and *enhypostasis*, see CD I/2, 162ff.,
216 (*anhypostasis* only); and IV/2, 49–50. See also Eberhard Jüngel, *God's Being Is in
Becoming: The Trinitarian Being of God in the Theology of Karl Barth; A Paraphrase*
(Edinburgh: T&T Clark, 2001), 96–97.
95. Webster, *Barth's Moral Theology*, 89.
96. CD IV/3, 713.
97. CD IV/3, 714.

this history in a way that many accounts that tend in a universalist direction do not.

This life of Jesus underscores the importance of time, decision, and lived life for humans; a principle removes such significance. It is essential here to be reminded of Barth's understanding of the positive relationship between eternity and time, according to which eternity does not remove time. I have offered a detailed study of this elsewhere,[98] and space here affords only a few extremely brief comments. Eternity does not remove the integrity of any moment of time or of eternity but unites and perfects them in simultaneity. To suggest that an account of universalism must sew up time and history into a singular "triumph of grace" through election is to misunderstand both eternity and the election of Jesus Christ. The election of Jesus Christ is an election of time in the life and particularity of Jesus: "The eternal divine decision as such has as its object *and content the existence of this one created being the man Jesus of Nazareth, and the work of this man in His life and death,* His humiliation and exaltation, His obedience and merit. It tells us further that in and with the existence of this man the eternal divine decision has as its object and content the execution of the divine covenant with man, the salvation of all men."[99] One misses the radicality of Barth's statement here if one fails to see the spatiotemporal particularity of this life and its form in death and resurrection. To misunderstand eternity is to

<hr/>

98. See Greggs, "Order and Movement of Eternity." See also *CD* II/1, §31.3, "The Eternity and Glory of God," as well as paragraphs on time at *CD* I/2, §14 and *CD* III/1, §51. For the most thorough discussion of this, see Richard H. Roberts, *A Theology on Its Way? Essays on Karl Barth* (Edinburgh: T&T Clark, 1991), esp. chap. 1. In this, Roberts engages in a thorough and fierce criticism of Barth on time, concluding that Barth is ultimately "ambiguous" and seeing the dissolution of time by eternity in Barth's theory. While Roberts is undoubtedly correct in the emphasis he places on these concepts in Barth's theology and identifies the very inner logics of Barth's work, his overall conclusions cannot be accepted. For a concise and clear critique of Roberts, see Bruce D. Marshall, "Review of Richard Roberts, *A Theology on Its Way? Essays on Karl Barth*," *Journal of Theological Studies* 44 (1993): 453–58.

99. *CD* II/2, 116, emphasis added.

fail to grasp the particularity involved in the statement "Jesus is Victor"—a particularity that can never be involved in a dogmatic principle of universal salvation, and one in which all temporal human particularities subsist. It is also to fail to see that there are few theologians who allow for so much time for humanity as Barth does. A principle of ultimate universal salvation may well dissolve or negate time, since everything has been sewn up from the start; but the life in time of the human person Jesus cannot justify such an account. It is necessary to reject any form of theology that removes temporality (as principles of universalism can), but this in no way needs to limit the ultimate victory of Christ.

Indeed, the issue of ultimacy itself requires further comment. In dealing with the eschaton, one is dealing with that which is ultimate; in dealing with human history as it is currently and subjectively experienced, one is faced with that which is penultimate. Each requires the other, and it is important to attend to each theologically. But the ultimate is always that—ultimate.[100] The freedom of humanity, the importance of obedience and faith, the significance of the church, and the continued existence of history and world-occurrence belong to the penultimate. Accounts that suggest a universal extent of salvation allow for this distinction and the significance of the penultimate, but the ultimate is still ultimate. It is as that which is penultimate that one is to understand the existence of the Christian "in the final manifestation of Jesus Christ. There can be no doubt, however, that in the liberation which comes to the Christian here and now, in that which is personally and specifically disclosed and given him in and with his calling, the Christian himself is not the end of the ways of God but only the preliminary sign of this end."[101]

---

100. See Bonhoeffer's discussion of the relationship between the ultimate and the penultimate. Dietrich Bonhoeffer, *Ethics*, Dietrich Bonhoeffer Works, vol. 6 (Minneapolis: Fortress, 2005), 153–70.

101. *CD* IV/3, 675.

Present-day Christian faith is not an ultimate decisive factor in and for the eschaton but a "preliminary sign of this end." Moreover, this sign is one "not only in anticipation of its own awaited completion but also in anticipation of what is truly and finally purposed in what God has done and revealed in Jesus Christ, namely, the liberation of all men."[102] The Christian is a penultimate sign of the ultimate, but the Christian cannot be understood as ultimately distinct or separate from the non-Christian.[103] Faith must never be seen as ultimate: "[in] the recognition of faith we are speaking of most important penultimate things, but not of ultimate things."[104] Penultimacy allows room for human freedom, decision, and the exercise of human will in history. This is a history that is real and valid in its penultimacy. In it there is room for faith, just as in it there is room for the possibility of rejection, condemnation, and unbelief. But these things are not ultimate; the victory of Jesus Christ is ultimate. We are led to this victory through the crescendo of human history. Jesus's victory does not drown out, remove, or sew up human history. Jesus's life is, instead, the basis for human history—not simply through some single moment in a pretemporal eternity that renders all the notes of history meaningless, but through a lived life culminating in crucifixion and resurrection, in which all of humanity is elected.[105] The reality of rejection as a possibility is there, indeed uncomfortably so (see above).[106] However, rejection is also elected *in* Christ in the crucifixion. This rejection is not ultimate; the verdict of the Father is seen in resurrection.[107] To claim that the penultimacy of rejection makes it

---

102. *CD* IV/3, 675.

103. *CD* IV/3, 351–52.

104. *CD* IV/1, 767.

105. Here one should see the reason for Barth's emphatic use of the biblical term "covenant." God is the covenantal God—the God of history.

106. *CD* II/2, §35.2 and 35.4.

107. See *CD* IV/1, §59.3. For this connection, see also *CD* II/2, 558, as well as Barth's thesis at §39: "He judges us as in His Son's death He condemns all our action as transgression, and by His Son's resurrection pronounces us righteous" (*CD* II/2, 733).

unreal is tantamount to the suggestion that the penultimacy of the cross makes it unreal. Both are necessary in the correct order, and neither undoes the reality of the other. So, too, the penultimacy of human rejection cannot undo the ultimacy of God's election; yet this does not undermine the reality of either penultimate or ultimate. A theology that seeks to move in a universalist direction has to attend to discussions of judgment and condemnation and to the threat of hell, rejection, and the abyss as realities in human existence.[108] But such a theology has to attend to these as to that which is penultimate. Here we can see what distinguishes the unbeliever and the believer: the unbeliever fears that these things are ultimate; the Christian trusts that Jesus is Victor.

Attendant Further Themes

Thus far, this chapter has argued that Barth's theology might have positive implications for and provide helpful limits to contemporary accounts of universalism. The first section considered the logics of Barth's account of election and pointed to the deeply particularist approach to universalism that a universalist theology seeking to draw on Barth must have. The second section considered the limit case on speech about universalism—that theology should address not universalism but Jesus Christ who is the Victor, and what the implications of this might be for the life of the believer. This final section seeks to consider, in relation to this deep particularism, three attendant themes that a theology tending in a universalist direction and seeking to draw on Barth's work must address: sin and unbelief, conversion, and the work of the Spirit in creating the particularity of the people of God. These are themes that any account of universalism must consider and themes that Barth's theology helps to unpack.

108. These are present in Barth, and rightful attention is paid to them in Bettis, "Is Karl Barth a Universalist?" and in Colwell, "Contemporaneity of the Divine Decision."

The Significance of Sin and Unbelief

Certain forms of universalism might be considered to arise from optimistic accounts of human capacity: the innate goodness of creation, the capacity of humans to choose ultimately in favor of God, and so forth. These accounts may well seem to underemphasize the seriousness of sin and the justice of God. We have already addressed this issue in relation to the election of reprobation by God in Jesus Christ (see above), but further comment on the universality of sin in the time following the crucifixion and resurrection of Christ requires comment. The very universality of sin, and crucially the very universality of sin as unbelief, may well form part of the basis for an account of universal salvation. Barth is clear that sin is unbelief: "Man's sin *is* unbelief in the God who was 'in Christ reconciling the world to himself,' who in Him elected and loved man from all eternity, who in Him created him, whose word to man from and to all eternity was and will be Jesus Christ."[109] Crucially, this sin is something that haunts the Christian at every point. In faith, there still exists "ambivalence, impotence, confusion and peril."[110] Christians are "the children of God by faith in Jesus Christ."[111] But this faith is described by Barth in relation to his actualistic logic: it is something that is *ever new* and *ever threatened*. Hence, Barth writes, "Faith is a new act each day and hour, *at war each day and hour with newly insurgent unbelief.* Thus Christians, in Luther's words, have never become but are always *becoming.*"[112] The simple binary categorization of believer/unbeliever does not work here. The Christian, too (and perhaps especially), stands under the judgment brought upon her by her unbelief. Perhaps Barth's most famous popular remarks on this are those he made in relation to the atheism of Max Bense: "I know the rather sinister figure of the

109. CD IV/1, 415, emphasis added.
110. CD IV/4, 150.
111. Karl Barth, *The Christian Life: Church Dogmatics*, vol. 4, part 4: *Lecture Fragments* (Edinburgh: T&T Clark, 1981), 78.
112. Barth, *Christian Life*, 78.

'atheist' very well, not only from books, but also because it lurks somewhere inside me too."[113] No clear line can be drawn between Christians and non-Christians on Barth's account, but this is not simply because of the grace and love of God for all humanity. This lack of a binary arises also from the faithless propensities of Christians. The Christian faith is the enactment of the cry, "I believe; help my unbelief!" (Mark 9:24).[114] An account of the breadth of salvation should, in part, arise from an acknowledgment of the failings of Christians, and thus account for faith in this context.[115]

Conversion in Christ

The acknowledgment of the Christian's sharing in sin is significant in terms of the negative association of the Christian with the unbeliever. But what of the positive side of faith, the decision to follow Christ? What are we to make of conversion?[116] Does the urgency of the gospel and the importance of the decision of faith mean little given the account of salvation offered in sections one and two? Can there be no meaningful speech about the significance of conversion?

Here there are four observations to make. First, conversion in the negative sense of conversion away from sin is accomplished *by Christ, in Christ* on the cross. This is the fulfillment of the verdict of God on humanity—the No of God spoken against Jesus on the cross because of human sinfulness.[117] This in turn leads (positively) to forgiveness of the human, which bespeaks "a judicial act in which God has maintained His glory in relation to man."[118]

113. Karl Barth, *Fragments Grave and Gay* (London: Collins, 1971), 45–46.
114. Barth often quotes this verse. E.g., *CD* I/1, 24; *CD* II/2, 337; *CD* IV/1, 616, 699, 748; and *CD* IV/2, 138.
115. For more on this topic, see Greggs, "Pessimistic Universalism."
116. For a broader account of Barth's engagement with Pietism (read, for an English-speaking audience, "evangelicalism"), see Eberhard Busch, *Karl Barth and the Pietists: The Young Karl Barth's Critique of Pietism and Its Response* (Downers Grove, IL: InterVarsity, 2004).
117. *CD* IV/1, 93.
118. *CD* IV/1, 94.

Second, conversion in the positive sense concerns the *sanctification* of the human; indeed, this is the dominant way in which Barth speaks of conversion. Again, in this account, conversion is achieved by Christ, in Christ:

> The sanctification of man which has taken place in this One is their sanctification. But originally and properly it is the sanctification of Him and not of them. Their sanctification is originally and properly His and not theirs. For it was in the existence of this One, in Jesus Christ, that it really came about, and is and will be, that God Himself became man, that the Son of God became also the Son of Man, *in order to accomplish in His own person the conversion of man to Himself*, his exaltation from the depth of his transgression and consequent misery, his liberation from his unholy being for service in the covenant, and therefore his sanctification.[119]

Since sanctification is, first and foremost, objectively fulfilled in Jesus Christ, sanctification and the conversion of the human to God is "effective and authoritative for all, and therefore for each and every man, and not merely for the people of God, the saints."[120]

Third, this work of sanctification and conversion, and its universal scope for humanity, is related to election. Under the discussion of conversion, Barth states of Christ, "He is what He is in this unique and incomparable and inimitable fashion as the One who is elected by God and Himself elects as God, the One in whom the decision has been made concerning all men, in whom they have been set in covenant with God and therefore ordained for conversion to Him."[121] Conversion to God rests in the eternal covenant with God in the eternal election of God in Jesus Christ.

Fourth, this does not mean that conversion is simply de jure, or passive. There is an *active* form of life that corresponds to an active participation in the sanctification of Christ. This terminates

119. CD IV/2, 514, emphasis added.
120. CD IV/2, 518.
121. CD IV/2, 515.

in a "real happening which takes place to men here and now in time and on earth."[122] Conversion is not, for Barth, a one-off, singular event; it is, instead, the whole of the life of faith, an ongoing movement of conversion in which the Christian finds herself.[123] Thus, conversion can still have a significant place even in a theology that seeks to articulate the salvific work of God for all people, but this understanding of conversion is itself grounded in the person and work of Christ.

The Work of the Spirit in Establishing the Particularity of the Believer[124]

The person of faith is able to participate actively in the work of Christ in the present, contingent condition of human history through the work of the Spirit in their individual life and in the life of the church. The importance of this cannot be underestimated for an account of salvation that tends in a universalist direction.[125] The work of the Spirit ensures that the account of salvation is not so objective as to render the experience of salvation in the life of the believer here and now as meaningless. The presence of the Spirit (rather than singularly the objective work of Christ in salvation or the election of humanity in Christ) is the condition for the being of a Christian.[126] Indeed, Barth writes,

> The being of man reconciled with God in Jesus Christ is reflected in the existence of the Christian. That is something we cannot

122. *CD* IV/2, 553.
123. *CD* IV/2, 470.
124. For a more thoroughgoing account of this, see Greggs, *Barth, Origen, and Universal Salvation*, chap. 5.
125. The work of the Holy Spirit provides a resolution to the tension Berkouwer suggests in Barth's doctrine of election between universal election and human decision (*Triumph of Grace*, 288).
126. Buckley summarizes this well when he states that the work of the Spirit is to universalize what is particular to Christ and to particularize the universality of Christ in a community of difference. James J. Buckley, "A Field of Living Fire: Karl Barth on the Spirit and the Church," *Modern Theology* 10 (1994): 81–102, at 92–93.

say of others. *It is not that they lack Jesus Christ and in Him the being of man reconciled to God. What they lack is obedience to His Holy Spirit,* eyes and ears and hearts which are open to Him, experience and knowledge of the conversion of man to God which took place in Him, the new direction which must correspond to the new being given to them in Him, life in and with His community, a part in its ministry, the confession of Him and witness to Him as its Lord and as the Head of all men.[127]

Non-Christians do not lack the work of reconciliation that God achieves in Christ; non-Christians lack the presence of the Holy Spirit in their lives and obedience to Him. In the present, this presence of the Spirit in the life of the believer, actualizing the reality of salvation in the contingent contemporaneity of human existence, is the distinguishing factor for the Christian. Even so, the Christian is distinguished as a *representative* of and for the rest of humanity.[128] Christian particularity is grounded in the presence of the Spirit, but not even this divides the saved from the damned absolutely: "He [the Spirit] makes them Christians. He divides them from non-Christians. But He also unites them with non-Christians. He is the promise which is given them, and He sets them in the position of hope. He gives them the power to wait daily for the revelation of what they already are, of what they became on the day of Golgotha."[129]

The Christian identifies with the world insomuch as those in the world are those for whom the promise is *yet* to be completely fulfilled, but the Christian is also the one who presently has the promise and as such is given "hope."[130] Again, this finds its outworking

127. *CD* IV/1, 92–93, emphasis added.
128. *CD* IV/1, 120.
129. *CD* IV/2, 330.
130. McDowell expresses this unity for Barth in terms of a "practical hope," which—in contrast to Marxist critiques—is less concerned with the believer's own individual redemption and more concerned with the telos of all. See John C. McDowell, *Hope in Barth's Eschatology: Interrogations and Transformations beyond Tragedy* (Aldershot, UK: Ashgate, 2001), 188ff. Rogers helpfully sees how Barth's

in relation to election.[131] The particularity of the elect—of those whose lives are part of the *movement* of God toward humanity in the event of Christ's election, a movement to which humans are called to respond—is found in the presence of the Spirit in their lives.[132] Christians are those who, as such, know their calling to the "objectively necessary expression of their election."[133] As Barth emphatically puts it, the Spirit is the One through whom the human's "election is accomplished in their life" (*zur Vollstreckung ihrer Erwählung in ihrem Leben*).[134] By the work of the Spirit, Christians testify to their election through a life of service in the world in response to the loving-kindness of God in the election of Jesus Christ.[135] It is the Spirit who enables humans to recognize the work of atonement and allows them to be "touched" by God and to live in response to this.[136]

Conclusion

Any theologian indebted to Barth who seeks, in the contemporary context, to offer a theology that tends in a universalist direction

doctrine of election should lead the Christian to the question of that to which the Holy Spirit calls her, grounded in a unity with the non-Christian. See Eugene F. Rogers Jr., "The Eclipse of the Spirit in Karl Barth," in *Conversing with Barth*, ed. John C. McDowell and Mike Higton (Aldershot, UK: Ashgate, 2001), 66–67.

131. Colwell correctly states, "The work of the Holy Spirit is no more an addendum to the completed work of the Son than the work of the Son is an addendum to the eternal decision of the Father" ("Contemporaneity of the Divine Decision," 158–59). See also Rogers, "Eclipse of the Spirit," 57ff.

132. Rosato states that there is an "ontological connection" (*ein ontologischer Zusammenhang*) independent of the human's noetic understanding of it but that it is only through the Spirit that the human can accept his "ontic belonging" (*die seinsmässige Zugehörigkeit*). Philip J. Rosato, *The Spirit as Lord: The Pneumatology of Karl Barth* (Edinburgh: T&T Clark, 1981), 123.

133. *CD* II/2, 345. It is important to note that knowing, in Barth's thought, comprises acknowledging (*anerkennen*), recognizing (*erkennen*), and confessing (*bekennen*). See, e.g., *CD* IV/1, 740ff. See also McDowell, *Hope in Barth's Eschatology*, 216–17.

134. *CD* II/2, 348; cf. *KD* II/2, 383.

135. *CD* II/2, 414. This is a theme that Barth builds on in *CD* IV.

136. *CD* IV/1, 148.

will offer an account of Barth's doctrine of election in order to determine the inner logics of the scope of salvation. However, such an account will again and again point back both to the particularity of the person of Jesus Christ and to the subjective particularity of those who seek to live lives that correspond to his. In addition to emphasizing particularism in this way, any account of universalism that draws on Barth will provide a strong account of divine sovereignty, and it will always stop short of uncritically presenting universalism as some kind of metaphysical principle.

This chapter has not sought to weigh in one way or the other on the question of whether Barth was himself a universalist; indeed, it has suggested that this might be the wrong way to pose the question. Instead, it has sought to draw on Barth's theology in order to bring into relief themes that a theologian who is in dialogue with Barth might wish to consider in constructing a theology that seeks to emphasize the ultimate victory of Jesus Christ. Throughout this chapter, it has been argued that any post-Barthian account of universalism has to be deeply particularist, accounting for salvation as arising from the life, death, and resurrection of Jesus Christ—from *this* life, death, and resurrection to which Christ is determined for all eternity in the eternal election of God to be God in Jesus Christ, to be the God of the salvation of humankind. It is in this life, death, and resurrection that we humans have our own election; in this is our hope and our particularity, whether we are believers or unbelievers. Barth's theology is the theology of the gospel—the good news for all humanity. The role of the theologian after Barth is to continue to proclaim the goodness of that good news for all the world.

4

Existential Universalism

David W. Congdon

Most accounts of Christian universalism share with Christian non-universalism the assumption that the goal of the Christian life is found in a glorious postmortem existence, either in some empyrean abode or Edenic earth. The question is whether all humans—or all animals, human and nonhuman—will enjoy this blessed existence, or only some. The end itself is not in dispute, only the extent of its embrace. Existential universalism, as I am calling it, offers an alternative account, however, one that remains agnostic at best about conscious postmortem existence and instead locates the meaning of universalism in the extent of God's this-worldly presence. Like existential theology more generally, existential universalism refuses to speculate about issues beyond the present existential encounter between God and the human person. Matters about the cosmic future—life after death or the end of the universe—are as irrelevant

to theology as matters about the cosmic past, such as how the
universe began or how life started on earth. Theologians have already made peace with handing over the cosmic past to scientists;
they should do the same with the cosmic future. What remains
is the present, the eternal moment of each breath, in which we
experience, or fail to experience, the hallowing presence of God.
Existential universalism is not concerned with where *we* end up
after we die; it is concerned rather with where *God* is active here
and now. Existential universalism argues that God is universally
present, not in the generic, anodyne sense of divine omnipresence,
but in the specifically saving sense of divine reconciliation.

In addition to the challenge posed by Christian nonuniversalism, existential universalism must also face the more immediate
problem of defending the universality of grace within an existential account of theology, which typically denies all universalism in
principle. The case of Rudolf Bultmann—the twentieth-century
champion of existential theology—and Karl Barth is instructive in
this regard. In their later years the two of them debated the interpretation of Romans 5, one of the key exegetical battlegrounds for
universalism, with Barth publishing *Christ and Adam according
to Romans 5* in 1952 and Bultmann responding with "Adam and
Christ according to Romans 5" in 1959.[1] Barth interpreted the
text in a strongly universalist direction, using Romans 5:12–21
as the interpretive key for the whole chapter. Bultmann, in his
response, criticized Barth's exegetical decision and used Romans
5:1–11 instead as his key. At the heart of Bultmann's interpretation of Paul was the existential question: Where is life (i.e., salvation, righteousness, grace, God) present? Bultmann charged Barth
with ignoring this question and focusing instead on "the rela-

1. See Karl Barth, *Christus und Adam nach Röm. 5: Ein Beitrag zur Frage nach
dem Menschen und der Menschheit* (Zollikon-Zürich: Evangelischer Verlag, 1952);
Rudolf Bultmann, "Adam und Christus nach Römer 5," *Zeitschrift für die Neutesta-
mentliche Wissenschaft* 50 (1959): 145–65. The English quotations in this chapter
from these and all other German sources are my own translations.

tionship between the human person and Christ," a relationship
that Barth expounded using the second half of Romans 5, which
Bultmann found to be thoroughly gnostic and virtually unusable.[2]
According to Bultmann, the whole Adam-Christ parallel that Paul
used in Romans 5:12–21, with its concept of "two humanities" or
"two human epochs," was "a gnostic idea conceived in terms of
cosmology, not salvation history."[3] Logically, this contrast would
have to mean that just as all people were subject to death after
Adam, so too "after Christ all people received life." But Bultmann immediately added, "Naturally that is not what Paul means;
rather, all people now stand before the decision whether they want
to belong to the λαμβάνοντες [those who receive]."[4] Bultmann saw
Paul articulating an existential gospel in the first half of Romans
5 and argued that the universal cosmic schema in the second half
was an alien concept that Paul was borrowing to make his point,
albeit in a clumsy and inadequate manner. Barth, however, used
the cosmic schema to support his universalizing Christology and,
precisely as Bultmann claimed, brushed aside the existential concern of the text—namely, to reassure the Roman followers of Jesus.
Barth asked the universalist question: Are all people included in
God's redemption? Bultmann asked the existentialist question: Is
God present in my life?

The challenge of existential universalism is to answer both questions at the same time, and the task of this chapter is to provide,
in brief, a theological argument for how that is possible.[5] The
result may not be attractive or persuasive—this could be a position of one—but the aim is to show that universalism is a much
more flexible category than its detractors often make it out to be.[6]

2. Bultmann, "Adam und Christus," 151.
3. Bultmann, "Adam und Christus," 154–55.
4. Bultmann, "Adam und Christus," 158.
5. I make the argument at much greater length in David W. Congdon, *The God
Who Saves: A Dogmatic Sketch* (Eugene, OR: Cascade Books, 2016).
6. The most impressive and egregious example of the reductive dismissive-
ness common among universalism's detractors is the recent two-volume work by

Living without the Afterlife

Some readers may dismiss this effort up front on the grounds that universalism without the promise of a conscious postmortem existence is meaningless to them. Certain proposals are a bridge too far for some people, and that is unavoidable. Others may already deny the idea of an afterlife and do not think the purpose of faith is to provide assurance about what will happen after death; readers who fall in this camp may safely skip this section. Still others, however, may simply wonder on what basis I deny the necessity of an afterlife and need an explanation before continuing. The purpose of this section, therefore, is to help people in this last camp understand why I do not regard the afterlife as an article of faith.[7]

The reasons to disbelieve in a conscious afterlife with final destinations—such as heaven and hell—fall into three categories: neuropsychological, historical, and theological. I treat them in this order for no particular reason. Some, like myself, will find the psychological arguments so compelling that arguments in the other categories simply provide further confirmation; others will demand intratheological arguments regarding such metaphysical questions. Those in the latter camp will likely not find anything sufficient to change their minds, particularly since there can be no definitive proof about the afterlife one way or the other. Belief in a postmortem existence is not something we are argued into, and it is unlikely that most people will be argued out of it. But that is precisely what the cognitive science research explains.

Turning first to this relatively new area of research, there is a significant body of literature in cognitive science and neuropsychology

---

Michael J. McClymond, *The Devil's Redemption: A New History and Interpretation of Christian Universalism*, 2 vols. (Grand Rapids: Baker Academic, 2018). McClymond argues that Christian universalism, in all its diversity, stems from a single "gnostic-esoteric" root.

7. An earlier version of my argument against the afterlife can be found in Congdon, *The God Who Saves*, 263–74.

exploring the natural origins of afterlife beliefs. Belief in some kind of afterlife is a recurrent feature in almost every human culture and religious community, which suggests "that humans have an intuitive tendency to understand death as the continuity of existence."[8] Jesse M. Bering developed a pioneering experiment to investigate how people conceive of dead persons' minds immediately after death. Whereas previous studies examined the reasons *why* people believe in an afterlife—usually focusing on wish fulfillment and anxiety about death—Bering examined *how* people conceive of the afterlife, in an attempt to discern a cognitive, precultural basis for this belief.[9] After multiple studies repeated by different researchers with different subjects, Bering concluded that psychological immortality is a "cognitive default" but that "culture develops and decorates the innate psychological building blocks of religious belief."[10]

8. Vera Pereira, Rodrigo de Sá-Saraiva, and Luís Faísca, "Immortality of the Soul as an Intuitive Idea: Towards a Psychological Explanation of the Origins of Afterlife Beliefs," *Journal of Cognition and Culture* 12, nos. 1–2 (2012): 101–27, at 102.

9. An earlier study of eighty-five Australian undergraduates by Michael Thalbourne found that belief in an afterlife correlated positively with the desire for an afterlife, adherence to some kind of dualism, and low anxiety about death. See Michael A. Thalbourne, "Belief in Life after Death: Psychological Origins and Influences," *Personality and Individual Differences* 21, no. 6 (1996): 1043–45.

10. Jesse M. Bering, "The Folk Psychology of Souls," *Behavioral and Brain Sciences* 29, no. 5 (2006): 453–62, at 454; Jesse Bering, *The Belief Instinct: The Psychology of Souls, Destiny, and the Meaning of Life* (New York: Norton, 2011), 123. For the articles on the earlier experiments, see Jesse M. Bering, "Intuitive Conceptions of Dead Agents' Minds: The Natural Foundations of Afterlife Beliefs as Phenomenological Boundary," *Journal of Cognition and Culture* 2, no. 4 (2002): 263–308; Jesse M. Bering and David F. Bjorklund, "The Natural Emergence of Reasoning About the Afterlife as a Developmental Regularity," *Developmental Psychology* 40, no. 2 (2004): 217–33; Jesse M. Bering, Carlos Hernandez Blasi, and David F. Bjorklund, "The Development of Afterlife Beliefs in Religiously and Secularly Schooled Children," *British Journal of Developmental Psychology* 23, no. 4 (2005): 587–607; Paul Harris and Marta Giménez, "Children's Acceptance of Conflicting Testimony: The Case of Death," *Journal of Cognition and Culture* 5, no. 1 (2005): 143–64; Rita Astuti and Paul L. Harris, "Understanding Mortality and the Life of the Ancestors in Rural Madagascar," *Cognitive Science* 32, no. 4 (2008): 713–40. Bering's experiment was replicated with Chinese undergraduate students to test the potential influence of a largely materialist cultural context, which yielded results similar to Bering's

Several different theories have been proposed to explain this intuitive belief in immortal souls and the afterlife. The most common explanation posits a connection between belief in the afterlife and anxiety about death, a position known as terror management theory (TMT), which stems originally from the work of Ernest Becker and was developed by Jeff Greenberg, Tom Pyszczynski, and Sheldon Solomon.[11] One problem with relying on this theory to explain belief in an afterlife, however, is that children as young as four—generally too young to fully comprehend death—have demonstrated seemingly dualistic beliefs. Bering's alternative is what he calls the simulation constraint theory. We are constrained by the limits of our experience, and thus we cannot know what it is like to be dead. For this reason, when we imagine or simulate postmortem existence, we are most likely to attribute to dead persons those psychological states that are most difficult to imagine being without (e.g., desiring and thinking), as opposed to those states that we have some experience being without (e.g., seeing and eating). The problem with this theory, as K. Mitch Hodge has shown, is that the simulation constraint should apply to prelife just as it applies to postlife. We should expect to find that belief in previous lives, such as in reincarnation traditions, is just as common as belief in continued existence after death. But the evidence does not show this. Furthermore, Bering's experiments show that

studies. See Junwei Huang, Lehua Cheng, and Jing Zhu, "Intuitive Conceptions of Dead Persons' Mentality: A Cross-Cultural Replication and More," *International Journal for the Psychology of Religion* 23, no. 1 (2013): 29–41.

11. See the discussion of the "terror of death" in Ernest Becker, *The Denial of Death* (New York: Free Press, 1973), 11–24. In his earlier work Becker talks about the "experience of anxiety" (including "annihilation anxiety") as a key element in the psychological development of children. See Ernest Becker, *The Birth and Death of Meaning: An Interdisciplinary Perspective on the Problem of Man*, 2nd ed. (New York: Free Press, 1971), 41–44. For the later theoretical development of TMT, see Jeff Greenberg et al., "Evidence for Terror Management Theory II: The Effects of Mortality Salience on Reactions to Those Who Threaten or Bolster the Cultural Worldview," *Journal of Personality and Social Psychology* 58, no. 2 (1990): 308–18; Sheldon Solomon, Jeff Greenberg, and Tom Pyszczynski, "Return of the Living Dead," *Psychological Inquiry* 8, no. 1 (1997): 59–71.

we believe intuitively in the continued existence of others, but the simulation constraint theory explains only belief in our own personal immortality.[12]

Hodge proposes a three-part theory that explains intuitive afterlife beliefs. First, he takes up an idea discussed by Bering called offline social reasoning, which is the ability to imagine that others are engaged in social activity when we are not able to observe them (i.e., offline). Bering views this as a secondary process that supports simulation constraint, but Hodge argues it is the origin of afterlife beliefs. This is because of Hodge's second thesis— namely, that "afterlife beliefs are social in nature."[13] These beliefs are not self-centered but other-centered, concerned with the immortality of friends and family. Finally, the third part of his theory is that, because of offline social reasoning and the social nature of afterlife beliefs, people imagine others in the afterlife as embodied, and thus as able "to continue to fulfill their social obligations with the living."[14] By recognizing that intuitions about the afterlife are inherently social, Hodge is able to distinguish belief in the afterlife from mind-body dualism. He observes that none of the participants in the studies he examines conceived of a disembodied agent; they all instinctively described the dead in bodily and social terms.[15] When people imagine the afterlife, they imagine embodied, recognizable persons.

Psychological research overwhelmingly points toward the conclusion that belief in an afterlife is a natural part of our cognitive evolution, but this is only the first aspect of the interdisciplinary challenge to the traditional religious account of such belief. The second comes from research in anthropology and the history of

12. K. Mitch Hodge, "Why Immortality Alone Will Not Get Me to the Afterlife," *Philosophical Psychology* 24, no. 3 (2011): 395–410, at 397–400.
13. K. Mitch Hodge, "On Imagining the Afterlife," *Journal of Cognition and Culture* 11, no. 3 (2011): 368.
14. Hodge, "On Imagining the Afterlife," 369.
15. See K. Mitch Hodge, "Descartes' Mistake: How Afterlife Beliefs Challenge the Assumption That Humans Are Intuitive Cartesian Substance Dualists," *Journal of Cognition and Culture* 8, no. 3 (2008): 387–415.

religions, which supports the work in psychology by demonstrating not only the universality of afterlife belief but also its diversity and development as part of cultural evolution. Scholars of the evolution of religion have demonstrated that belief in some kind of afterlife goes back to the earliest human cultures. In a study published in 2016, Hervey Peoples, Pavel Duda, and Frank Marlowe examined a global sample of thirty-three hunter-gatherer societies. They found that, after animism—the belief in the spiritual animation of all nature, which was found in every society—belief in the afterlife was tied with shamanism as the second-most common trait (79 percent).[16] They then developed a phylogenetic supertree and tested for the evolutionary development of these character traits. The study concluded that, while "animism is fundamental to religion," belief in the afterlife is "likely to have emerged first from the base of animistic beliefs."[17] Shamanism and ancestor worship develop as a result of a prior belief in the afterlife, rather than the other way around. If, as Hodge argues, the afterlife is a function of our social obligations, then it would make sense for shamans—who provide social cohesion in the face of uncertainty—and ancestor worship to develop in connection with the afterlife.[18]

Not only is belief in some kind of afterlife a near-universal feature of ancient religion, but the version of the afterlife found in hunter-gatherer groups is typically a kind of rebirth, one connected animistically to the natural cycles of death and new life and often involving little distinction between human and nonhuman animals.[19] According to Gananath Obeyesekere, over time certain

16. Hervey Peoples, Pavel Duda, and Frank Marlowe, "Hunter-Gatherers and the Origins of Religion," *Human Nature: An Interdisciplinary Biosocial Perspective* 27, no. 3 (2016): 261–82, at 267.

17. Peoples, Duda, and Marlowe, "Origins of Religion," 270, 272.

18. See Thomas T. Hills, "Masters of Reality," *Aeon*, November 1, 2018, https://aeon.co/essays/why-did-shamanism-evolve-in-societies-all-around-the-globe.

19. See Gananath Obeyesekere, *Imagining Karma: Ethical Transformation in Amerindian, Buddhist, and Greek Rebirth* (Berkeley: University of California Press, 2002), 19–71.

groups began a process of ethicization that resulted in seeing the afterlife as a place of reward or punishment, with different outcomes for different groups of people. The Tlingit, for example, have a heavenly location for those who die in war, a realm near earth for those who die naturally, and a hell-like place for those who commit wrongs.[20] In antiquity, ancient Egyptians and Persians were unique for their early versions of paradise and hell after death. By comparison, ancient Israel and ancient Greece viewed reward and punishment in terms of personal fame, the blessing of children, or the future prosperity of the nation. According to Sarah Iles Johnston, a revolution in the idea of the afterlife occurred in the Hellenistic period, beginning in the late sixth century BCE due to Pythagoras, the Orphics, and the mystery cults, which led to the idea of the immortality of the soul and to various mythical conceptions of the afterlife as a place of individual reward and punishment. These views then made their way into Second Temple Judaism and eventually into Christianity.[21]

The research in cognitive science and the history of religions suggests that the belief in the afterlife is not only a natural response to our social existence but also a cultural idea that has evolved due to contingent developments in philosophical and religious history. This explains the conflicting accounts of individual eschatology in the Jewish and Christian scriptures, which range from the period of southwest Asian antiquity, without an ethicized individual afterlife, to the Hellenistic Diaspora and the early Christian community, with its accounts of individual resurrection and damnation. This intracanonical tension is a key feature of the final, theological argument against the afterlife, whose main proponents in the twentieth century have been Karl Barth and Eberhard Jüngel. Barth draws heavily on the Hebrew scriptures in developing his position on the afterlife in §47 of his *Church Dogmatics*, where he

20. Obeyesekere, *Imagining Karma*, 76.
21. Sarah Iles Johnston, *Religions of the Ancient World: A Guide* (Cambridge, MA: Belknap, 2004), 470–71.

134   Varieties of Christian Universalism

discusses the question of human temporality. Human existence, according to the Hebrew Bible, is a temporally limited existence in contrast to the unlimited life of God. The prophets proclaim "a strict *opposition* between the temporally completed being of humanity in death on the one side and the temporally unlimited being of God on the other as the Lord not only of life but also of death and the underworld."[22] For this reason our only hope in death lies in the existence of God, not in a life beyond death: "The Old Testament says *nothing* of a renewal of human beings in a time after their death, of a continuation of their lives, of resurrection in this sense, and therefore of an eternal life granted to them."[23] When the Psalmist cries out for salvation, it is for a return to the land of the living, not for a life after death. Death is the completion of our existence, after which our lives are enclosed by God.

The New Testament scriptures, Barth argues, are fundamentally consistent with this vision, except now our hope as Christians is to have our life *in* and *with* Christ. The same contrast remains between God's eternal existence and humanity's temporal existence, but this divine existence is located in the person of Jesus Christ, in whom our life is now hidden (Col. 3:3). Eternal life does not mean our mortal lives are extended into an ongoing future but rather that our finished, mortal existence "puts on" immortality (1 Cor. 15:53). For this reason "there is no question of continuing into an unending future and in this future having a somehow altered life; what New Testament hope expects beyond human death is rather the 'eternalizing' of our *ending* life." Our past life undergoes a transformation and participates in God's eternal life, and *this* is what is meant by the resurrection of the dead.[24] Eberhard Jüngel furthers Barth's position by arguing that

22. Karl Barth, *Church Dogmatics*, ed. G. W. Bromiley and T. F. Torrance, 4 vols. (Edinburgh: T&T Clark, 1956–1975), III/2, 619, revised translation (rev.). Hereafter this work is cited as *CD*.
23. *CD* III/2, 618, rev.
24. *CD* III/2, 624, rev.

human beings are defined by the fact that they "have a *history*," a history that is of irreplaceable significance; our history has eternal value not because our lives are eternal but because we are related to the eternal God.[25] The temporal boundaries of our existence define our identity, and thus any conception of resurrection that abolishes these boundaries would abolish "the individuality of the life of a person."[26] Salvation does not mean we are saved *from* this life but rather that *this* particular life is saved: "Finite life will be *eternalized* as finite. But not through infinite extension—there is no immortality of the soul—but rather through participation in God's own life."[27]

While Barth was quite critical of Bultmann's existentialism, his position on the afterlife leads practically to the same conclusion: the hope of Christian faith is a *present* hope in God's grace here and now, not a hope in a better life to come. Barth grounds this hope in the past event of the historical Christ, whereas Bultmann grounds it in the present event of the kerygmatic Christ—but either way, one is compelled to embrace a kind of existential theology that replaces the question "Where are *we* after death?" with the question "Where is *God* in life?" Instead of asking where everyone will be when they die, existential theology asks where God is now in relation to each person, and existential universalism claims that God is savingly present to each person irrespective of their conscious confession of faith in Christ.

Unconscious Faith

Soteriologies, especially within the Protestant orbit, tend to fall into two categories: those that interpret salvation as an objective

25. Eberhard Jüngel, *Tod* (Stuttgart: Kreuz-Verlag, 1971), 148; English translation (ET), Eberhard Jüngel, *Death: The Riddle and the Mystery*, trans. Iain Nicol and Ute Nicol (Philadelphia: Westminster, 1975), 118.

26. Jüngel, *Tod*, 151 (ET 119).

27. Jüngel, *Tod*, 151–52 (ET 120).

reality independent of individual experience and those that interpret salvation as a subjective reality only actualized in each individual. The former stresses divine sovereignty and human depravity, while the latter stresses divine initiative and human participation, at least where the matter of salvation is concerned. Most versions of Christian universalism can be mapped onto one of these soteriological types. They either require all people to be included generally in God (e.g., in the humanity of Christ) or expect conversion to be an individual decision that occurs sometime in the afterlife. Universalisms of the first type are not existential, while those of the second type require a conscious afterlife as a condition for their possibility. Existential universalism proposes a different way of thinking about universal salvation, one that is fully existential and fully this-worldly. And developing this requires that one understand faith—a positive relation to God—as prelinguistic and unconscious.

Existential theology presupposes that there is no saving relationship with God apart from faith, and in that sense it stands in contrast to someone like Karl Barth, who separates the objective realization of salvation from its subjective actualization. The advantage of Barth's Reformed approach is that it more clearly preserves the Protestant conviction that faith is an act and not a work, which is itself an extension of the traditional Christian claim that faith is a gift of God. Faith on this view is not a human achievement by which we procure our redemption (e.g., a cognitive assent to doctrines about God or a libertarian choice to believe), since that would violate our justification by grace alone. In the language of Thomas Aquinas, faith is only possible when God "infuses" it in us and so raises us above our nature; faith is "God moving the human person inwardly by grace."[28] The objectivity of Barth's soteriology is an extension of this Augustinian tradition regarding the priority of divine grace, even though, as a

---

28. Thomas Aquinas, *Summa theologiae* II-II.2.3 ad 2; II-II.6.1 resp., my trans.

Protestant, Barth rejects the ontological metaphor of infusion in favor of the forensic language of imputation. The point remains the same: faith is only possible because God actualizes it in us. As a modern Reformed theologian, however, Barth radicalizes this understanding of grace so that an individual's subjective response of faith is not a precondition for one's reconciliation with God. The object of faith—the reconciling work of God in Christ— already has its existence, essence, and significance for the human subject "even without their faith and respect!" Faith, according to Barth, "does not realize or find anything new, but instead it finds what *is* already there for believers and unbelievers alike."[29] Existential universalism rejects Barth's bifurcation between the objective and subjective moments of reconciliation, with the subjective serving only to find what is already objectively present, but it shares Barth's position that the *conscious* act of faith does not have any saving significance. The alternative that existential universalism proposes is to understand faith as primarily and essentially *unconscious*, and for this we can draw on the work of Dietrich Bonhoeffer.

In *Act and Being*, his 1930 *Habilitationsschrift*, Bonhoeffer systematically elaborates on the distinction between *actus directus* and *actus reflexus*, which he draws from Franz Delitzsch's 1855 *System of Biblical Psychology*. Delitzsch uses this distinction to make sense of Paul's ostensibly opposed claims that, on the one hand, gentiles "do not know God [τὰ μὴ εἰδότα τὸν Θεόν]" (1 Thess. 4:5; Gal. 4:8) and, on the other hand, they "knew God [γνόντες τὸν Θεὸν]" (Rom. 1:21). Delitzsch explains this apparent contradiction by distinguishing between *actus directus*, meaning a simple, existentially direct action that does not rise to the level of consciousness, and *actus reflexus*, referring to a complex action of conscious reflection and internal acknowledgment. According to Delitzsch, "God truly gives Godself to all people in

29. CD IV/1, 742, rev.

God's works," and while this revelation is known by all people
actu directo, it is known *actu reflexo* only when there is an "inner
assent to this self-revelation of God" and a "free subjectifying
[*Subjectivirung*] of the objectively revealed divinity."[30] The *actus
directus* unconsciously knows that the Logos is "the light of all
people" that "enlightens everyone" (John 1:4, 9), while the *actus
reflexus* is the conscious rejection or acceptance of this light, such
as when "the world did not know him" and "his own people did
not accept him" (John 1:10–11). Delitzsch thus uses these terms
to rethink the distinction between God's objective, universal action and the human person's subjective response to it in terms of
two kinds of subjectivity—respectively, prereflective and reflective, or unconscious and conscious. The two actions correspond
to two kinds of faith. The *actus directus* is the essential form of
faith (*forma fidei essentialis*), the faith that justifies because it
depends wholly on the promise of God; the *actus reflexus* is the
self-reflective form of faith in which "we acknowledge our own
doing."[31] Delitzsch employs the *actus directus* to explain not only
the universality of revelation and salvation but also the effectiveness of the sacraments apart from the individual's reflective faith,
as in infant baptism. In so doing he connects these concepts to the
Protestant scholastic distinction between *fides directa* and *fides
reflexa*, which was developed for this very purpose.

Bonhoeffer picks up Delitzsch's conceptuality at this point to
further explore the role of consciousness and unconsciousness
in theological anthropology. The Protestant scholastic concept
of *fides directa*, he says, refers to "the act of faith that, while
completed in a person's consciousness, is not reflected in it. . . .
Clinging to Christ need not become conscious of itself, but rather
it is wholly taken up by the completion of the act itself." Those
who exist in Christ not only do not see their sin; they also do not

30. Franz Delitzsch, *System der biblischen Psychologie* (Leipzig: Dörffling und
Franke, 1855), 302.
31. Delitzsch, *System der biblischen Psychologie*, 307.

see their faith—or "even themselves."[32] The being of a person is wholly hidden in Christ (Col. 3:3), hidden as much from themselves as from anyone else. While the act of faith offers plenty for a person to consciously reflect on, Bonhoeffer's point is that this act "cannot be 'found' by reflection," because the act cannot be isolated from one's hidden being-in-Christ: "never in being without act, never in act without being."[33] To have our being in Christ is to be defined by the future, since the future is as hidden and ungraspable as our faith in Christ is. The unconscious act of *fides directa* thus places "the human person in the future of Christ" and actualizes "the eschatological possibility of the child." The baptized child, whose unreflective existence is entirely dependent on God, represents the act of *fides directa*, while the constantly reflective, analyzing, objectifying adult represents the act of *fides reflexa*. According to Bonhoeffer, *fides directa* is infant baptism, which is "letting-oneself-be-defined by the future," while *fides reflexa* is religiosity, which is defined by the sin and guilt of the past. Infant baptism becomes the paradigmatic form of unconscious, direct faith, since it marks the occurrence of revelation "without the reflective answer of consciousness."[34] As he put it in his 1932 notes on theological anthropology, "Faith [*Glaube*] means *actus directus*. Devoutness [*Gläubigkeit*] means *actus reflexus*."[35]

During his final days in the Tegel military prison, Bonhoeffer returned to these early ideas about faith and proposed the concept of "unconscious Christianity" (*unbewußtes Christentum*). The term was not unique to Bonhoeffer but originated with Richard Rothe's 1857 sermon on Mark 9:24 ("I believe; help my unbelief!"), "The Struggle between Belief and Unbelief in Jesus in

32. Dietrich Bonhoeffer, *Akt und Sein: Transzendentalphilosophie und Ontologie in der systematischen Theologie*, ed. Hans-Richard Reuter, Dietrich Bonhoeffer Werke 2 (Munich: Kaiser, 1988), 158.
33. Bonhoeffer, *Akt und Sein*, 23, 159.
34. Bonhoeffer, *Akt und Sein*, 159.
35. Dietrich Bonhoeffer, *Berlin: 1932–1933*, ed. Carsten Nicolaisen and Ernst-Albert Scharffenroth, Dietrich Bonhoeffer Werke 12 (Munich: Kaiser, 1997), 186.

the Hearts of the Children of Our Time."[36] Rothe's concept of
unconscious Christianity was rather different from Bonhoeffer's.
As Martin Rade observed in a November 1904 lecture, Rothe's
concept was rooted in his conviction that "the state is in fact for
him the religious-moral community" and thus "the church must
finally dissolve into the state."[37] For Rothe, unconscious Christianity means that people are born into a "Christian nation" and
thereby become Christian unawares.

Bonhoeffer means something radically different by the term.
For him, unconscious Christianity is a strictly *theological* idea,
not something natural, social, or cultural; it is a reality created
and revealed by God alone. A further indication of what Bonhoeffer means comes in a note he wrote in prison sometime in July to
August 1944: "Unconscious Christianity: Left [hand] doesn't know
what the right is doing. Matthew 25."[38] The reference to the parable of the sheep and goats suggests that unconscious Christians
are like those who did not know they were tending to the Son of
Man in caring for "the least of these." If we understand the Son
of Man here as Christ, or simply as God, then the "Christianity"
of unconscious Christians is not determined by their cultural contexts or social conditioning but instead by God's self-identification
with the least of these. This corresponds to Bonhoeffer's point in
Act and Being about *fides directa*: the relation to God that occurs
in direct faith is not an achievement of the person but wholly an
actuality established by God. The concept of unconscious Christianity is a way of highlighting the fact that this reality of being-
in-Christ, while determined by God, pertains to the individual
person. Bonhoeffer recognizes the implications of an unconscious
account of faith for the question of universal salvation. As an act

36. Richard Rothe, *R. Rothe's nachgelassene Predigten*, ed. Daniel Schenkel, 2
vols. (Elberfeld: Friderichs, 1869), 2:313–28, at 327.

37. Martin Rade, *Unbewußtes Christentum* (Tübingen: Mohr, 1905), 10.

38. Dietrich Bonhoeffer, *Widerstand und Ergebung: Briefe und Aufzeichnungen
aus der Haft*, ed. Christian Gremmels, et al., Dietrich Bonhoeffer Werke 8 (Gütersloh:
Kaiser, 1998), 547.

that is "never grasped in reflection" and even "eliminates itself," this direct, unconscious faith opens a perspective, he says, in which "not all paths appear closed to the eschatology of apokatastasis."[39] Existential universalism picks up where Bonhoeffer leaves off. The concept of unconscious faith provides the formal mechanism for conceiving of salvation outside the boundaries of conscious Christianity—the ecclesiastical institutions of word and sacrament, prayer and discipleship. The question is how to ground this account of faith theologically. What is the content of this mechanism? What is the basis for its saving power? Enlightenment accounts of natural religion grounded what we could call unconscious faith in human reason and conscience, in the "natural law" written into the fabric of existence and accessible to all people through their native faculties. Friedrich Schleiermacher sought to do greater justice to the reformational understanding of *iustitia aliena* with his concept of "feeling" (*Gefühl*), which stands in contrast to rational thought and moral action, both of which are achieved and actualized by the conscious individual. What he calls the "feeling of the infinite" in his speeches *On Religion* or the "feeling of absolute dependence" in his *Glaubenslehre* is universal in scope without requiring conscious fidelity to Christianity.[40] This religious feeling embraces the multitude of human beliefs and practices and "does not strive to bring those who believe and feel under a single faith and a single feeling."[41] More recent theologies of religious pluralism, such as John Hick's theory of salvation as "transformation from self-centredness to Reality-centredness," develop Schleiermacher's core insight in a way that respects the

39. Bonhoeffer, *Akt und Sein*, 160.
40. Friedrich Schleiermacher, *Über die Religion: Reden an die Gebildeten unter ihren Verächtern (1799)*, ed. Günter Meckenstock, Kritische Gesamtausgabe 1.2: *Schriften aus der Berliner Zeit, 1796–1799* (Berlin: de Gruyter, 1984), 217; Friedrich Schleiermacher, *Der christliche Glaube: Nach den Grundsätzen der evangelischen Kirche im Zusammenhange dargestellt (1830/31)*, ed. Rolf Schäfer, 2 vols., Kritische Gesamtausgabe 1.13 (Berlin: de Gruyter, 2003), §4, 39.
41. Schleiermacher, *Über die Religion*, 217.

irreducible diversity of religious practice and experience.[42] While Hick does not discuss unconscious faith, his approach recognizes that every person is at some stage in their spiritual development, and the purpose of religion, including Christianity, is not to demarcate who is in and who is out but instead to guide people further in their development, toward whatever it is that their religious context understands to be the goal of human existence. There is much to commend in Hick and Schleiermacher, among others, but the aim of this chapter is to sketch a theology of existential universalism that is distinctively *christological* in its grounding, focused less on religion in general and more on the internal norms of Christianity itself.

Existential Universalism and the Cross

The account of existential universalism I will develop here takes as its starting point the Pauline claim "I have been crucified with Christ; and it is no longer I who live, but it is Christ who lives in me" (Gal. 2:19–20).[43] It is worth pausing for a moment to reflect on the decision to emphasize crucifixion. As feminist and queer theologians have rightly pointed out, the default emphasis on the cross in Christian theology has often been injurious to the faith. Crucicentric theologies frequently presuppose and valorize the

---

42. John Hick, *A Christian Theology of Religions: The Rainbow of Faiths* (London: SCM, 1995), 107.

43. I construct this account of universalism around my reading of this verse not because of any inherent authority of the Bible, and certainly not in deference to some Pauline "canon within the canon," as if I understood myself bound as a theologian to develop my position on the basis of these texts. Unlike evangelical universalists, and more like the early Christian universalists, existential universalists arrive at their position not because the texts demand it but, rather, because a coherent and meaningful understanding of God demands that we read the texts this way. It would, theoretically, be possible to develop such a position using an entirely different set of religious texts—truth is truth wherever we find it—but this account is in conversation with the Christian tradition, so it makes sense to use the texts that have historically been central to the self-understanding of Christians. Whether they should remain so central is a question for another time.

myth of redemptive violence. Even if they avoid the crudest forms of "divine child abuse"—something that orthodox theologians dismiss, perhaps too quickly, by appealing to the simplicity and single subjectivity of the divine being—crucicentric theologies have still contributed to a religious atmosphere that sees suffering, torture, and death as necessary tools in achieving divine ends. This has become especially problematic in modern cross-centered trinitarian theology (e.g., Hans Urs von Balthasar, Jürgen Moltmann, Wolfhart Pannenberg, and Graham Ward), which has eternalized the cross as an event in the immanent trinity, such that, according to Linn Tonstad, "the Son's road to death, the death of God, becomes the crux and fulcrum of all revelation." Tonstad has critically analyzed how these theologies are not only "projectionist and incoherent," particularly those that project human sociality upon a social doctrine of the trinity, but also gendered and sexed in a way that grounds "the ultimacy of heterosexuality in the Christian imaginary."[44] Tonstad thus proposes a theology centered on resurrection that refuses the reduction of the Son's road to the cross to "(self-)sacrifice or expiation." Resurrection instead "symbolizes the outcome of his entire ministry: the final transformation of human persons through their rematerialization."[45] Resurrection, however, is not the mere restoring and securing of what was lost; instead, it gestures toward something ambiguous, apophatic, and fragile—a gift of a future self beyond the passing away of the present world.

The two key problems with crucicentric theologies, according to Tonstad, are thus the expiatory logic and the trinitarian projectionism. Neither are essential for Christian faith, much less for the kind of existential project proposed here. The cross does not satisfy some cruel cosmic equation by which human sin can be forgiven only through the slaughter of divinely innocent

44. Linn Marie Tonstad, *God and Difference: The Trinity, Sexuality, and the Transformation of Finitude* (New York: Routledge, 2016), 11.
45. Tonstad, *God and Difference*, 244.

blood, nor does the cross serve as the historical womb of the eternal trinity, birthing God's trinitarian differentiation through an act of torture and sacrifice. Freed from the need to serve as an atonement mechanism or as the ontological nodal point for God's triune being, the cross can serve a similarly fragile, multivalent meaning as the resurrection. Instead of being the "fulcrum of all revelation," it can serve a more humble role: not as a fulcrum upon which everything depends, but as a lens, one of many, that can focus revelation in particular ways.

One of these ways is found in liberation theologies that see in the crucified Jesus the identification of God with the impoverished of the world, or rather, as Enrique Dussel says, see the poor as "an epiphany of the crucified God appealing for help" and thus as "the necessary path of salvation."[46] Reworking Cyprian's classic *extra ecclesiam nulla salus* (outside the church there is no salvation), Jon Sobrino argues that *extra pauperes nulla salus* (outside the poor there is no salvation).[47] Ignacio Ellacuría thus argues for a historical soteriology that looks through the passion and crucifixion of Christ to the "crucified people" throughout history. The cross becomes the lens that discloses the world of the poor as the truth of the world—indeed, the truth of God.[48] James Cone similarly uses the cross as a lens by which to see the truth of the racial caste system in the United States and its violent practice of lynching.[49] A crucicentric liberationist theology does not valorize the cross as a necessary moment in God's providential plan for achieving salvation; on the contrary, it understands the cross as the revelation of where God's saving action has always

46. Enrique Dussel, "The Kingdom of God and the Poor," *International Review of Mission* 68, no. 270 (1979): 115–30, at 130.

47. Jon Sobrino, *No Salvation Outside the Poor: Prophetic-Utopian Essays* (Maryknoll, NY: Orbis Books, 2008), 35.

48. Ignacio Ellacuría, "The Crucified People: An Essay in Historical Soteriology [1978]," in *Ignacio Ellacuría: Essays on History, Liberation, and Salvation*, ed. Michael E. Lee (Maryknoll, NY: Orbis Books, 2013), 195–224.

49. James H. Cone, *The Cross and the Lynching Tree* (Maryknoll, NY: Orbis Books, 2011).

occurred—namely, among those abandoned and crucified by the world. The cross in this sense is the apocalypse, the revelatory unveiling, of the mystery of God's identification with the plight of human history.

Existential universalism exists in solidarity with these liberationist accounts of the cross while offering, naturally, a more universal account that accommodates other forms of God's identification with humanity. Without losing sight of God's preferential option for the poor—indeed, such an "option" is hardly optional but is essential to the love that is God's being—existential universalism seeks to clarify the myriad ways in which God is savingly present to the totality of creaturely life. Ellacuría is particularly helpful in pointing us in the right direction. He describes his account of the "crucified people" as the "principle of universal salvation," and he can do so because he develops a structural account of sin and salvation in which both refer fundamentally to collective bodies of people—indeed, to the totality of all people—and not to individuals.[50] Humanity is not divided into two cleanly distinguishable camps, the oppressors and the oppressed, with one group crucifying the other. Such a "Manichean division of the world" would "situate all good in the world on one side and all evil on the other." Rather, humans are enmeshed in systems and institutions of oppression that implicate everyone in various ways. The intersectionality of human identity means a person can be oppressed in one sense and an oppressor in another. Human history is a repeating pattern of "people crucifying others in order to live themselves," and thus "subsystems of crucifixion" exist among both oppressors and oppressed, constantly generating new relations of exploitation and suffering.[51] For this reason, as David Bentley Hart writes in reflection on Gregory of Nyssa, "there can be no true human unity, nor even any perfect unity between

50. Ellacuría, "Crucified People," 208.
51. Ellacuría, "Crucified People," 210.

God and humanity, except in terms of the concrete solidarity of all persons in that complete community that is, alone, the true image of God."[52] Each person is connected to every other person through the structures of human existence, and thus each person is indispensable to the work of redemption. No one can be saved unless everyone can be saved.

Having acknowledged the systemic interconnection of all people, Ellacuría admits that "the crucified people thus remains somewhat imprecise insofar as it is not identified, at least formally, with a specific group in history." But he goes on to identify the crucified people with "the third world, the oppressed classes, and those who struggle for justice, *insofar as* they are third world, oppressed class, and people who struggle for justice." While the category of "the oppressed class" remains somewhat in flux, Ellacuría draws a sharp line between the "third world" and the "first world": "the first world is not in this line [of historical continuity with the Suffering Servant], and the third world is."[53] This passage is indicative of most Latin American liberation theology, deriving as it does from a Roman Catholic theological framework in which the church is the "prolongation of the incarnation," a term that has dominated post-*ressourcement* ecclesiology.

The innovation of liberation theology was to shift the locus of this prolongation from the sacramental institution to the oppressed class, thereby redefining what counts as an extension of the incarnate Christ throughout history. This innovation has the advantage of making space for an unconscious account of faith, but it sits in uneasy tension with Ellacuría's recognition that subsystems of crucifixion pervade all worlds and societies. A clean division of "first" and "third," even if these are dynamic categories that are constantly in flux, is overly abstract. The question of salvation becomes the question of whether one belongs

52. David Bentley Hart, *That All Shall Be Saved: Heaven, Hell, and Universal Salvation* (New Haven: Yale University Press, 2019), 143.
53. Ellacuría, "Crucified People," 222.

to the class of the oppressed or the oppressors, but that question is difficult to answer without adequate criteria for determining whether and when one is part of one class or another. A simple division along the lines of economic class—to the exclusion of intersectional factors like gender, race, and sexuality—is hardly sufficient. The framework quickly degenerates into a dispute over identity classification. Furthermore, from a Protestant standpoint, there is the additional problem of collapsing the "crucified people" into a visible, objective community in which salvation is based on qualities *possessed* by the people. Whether these qualities are participation in a sacramental rite or identification with a particular class makes little difference. Either way, salvation becomes a matter of personal security, an objective status that one possesses by virtue of the correct outward action or external quality.

Finally, despite Ellacuría's claim that the "crucified people" is the "principle of universal salvation," it is difficult to understand quite how, on his terms, one arrives at a Christian universalism if the category itself depends on the division of the world into "first" and "third." Ellacuría ends his essay without answering this question, opting instead to acknowledge that the world's salvation will come when the crucified people are ultimately resurrected and pass judgment on the world. Presumably, then, universal salvation will occur when the oppressed of the earth end the division between classes. As he says in his later essay "The Historicity of Christian Salvation," "universal liberation" will occur when the poor are "liberated from their poverty" and the rich are "liberated from their wealth."[54] As important as this is as a social goal, tethering universal salvation to the objective achievement of a classless society simply replaces a transcendent afterlife with an immanent one and shifts the accomplishment of this universalism from divine to human agency.

54. Ignacio Ellacuría, "The Historicity of Christian Salvation [1984]," in *Ignacio Ellacuría*, 137–68, at 161.

Existential universalism does not compete with an emancipatory universalism any more than transcendence competes with immanence—and indeed, an existential universalism ought to point toward the social necessity of an immanent universalism along the lines of what Ellacuría describes. But existential universalism insists on an account of salvation as a transcendent divine act, an event that cannot be objectified within the world as one social configuration among others. Salvation is not an objective possession that grants existential and soteriological security to some to the exclusion of others. On the contrary, as I explore below, existential universalism understands salvation to be the event of our *desecuring*, and thus precisely for this reason what binds us in solidarity with others.

"It Is No Longer I Who Live": Salvation as Existential Cocrucifixion

Our starting point, as indicated above, is found in Paul's statement "I have been crucified with Christ; and it is no longer I who live, but it is Christ who lives in me" (Gal. 2:19–20). Such a claim seems highly puzzling to our ears today. If Paul is "crucified with Christ," then clearly crucifixion here cannot mean a crudely literal death with actual wood and nails. What is it that binds the individual Paul with the crucified Christ? As Troy Martin, Matthew Thiessen, and Paula Fredriksen have argued, Paul assumes that *pistis* (faith) enables one to receive the *pneuma* of Christ—*pneuma* being a cosmic material substance in the ancient Mediterranean world, the very substance of stars and angels, and not the nebulous, immaterial "spirit" of modern parlance. As Thiessen puts it, "The *pneuma* accompanies the message of Christ crucified and risen and penetrates those who hear it."[55] This penetration occurs,

---

55. Matthew Thiessen, *Paul and the Gentile Problem* (New York: Oxford University Press, 2016), 109.

according to Martin, possibly through the oronasal cavity.[56] When Paul elsewhere says that "our old self was crucified with him so that the body of sin might be destroyed" (Rom. 6:6), he is referring to the fact that "pneumatic infusion comes through immersion into Christ's death," an immersion that occurs in the act of baptism (Rom. 6:3–4).[57] Resurrection, for Paul, is the fulfillment of this infusion of *pneuma* and will occur when the initial foretaste of *pneuma* received through *pistis* finally becomes complete, thereby replacing the earthly, psychical body with the heavenly, pneumatic body (1 Cor. 15:40–44). The redeemed children of God will thus undergo a "process of astralization" and join Christ and the angels "up in the shining aether beyond the moon," where they will shine like the stars.[58] Crucially, these beliefs took shape in an environment of feverish apocalyptic expectation that anticipated the imminent arrival of God's cosmic reign and the vindication of the children of God.

All of this likely strikes readers today as bizarre, but that only underscores how foreign Paul and the other early Jesus followers are to us in the twenty-first century. Their concept of salvation has little meaning for people who understand that stars are gaseous spheres of thermonuclear reactions millions of light-years away and that our bodies are made of water and organic compounds that we share with other living organisms. We can only go *through* the strangeness of these texts, not around it. As historians of Second Temple Judaism have demonstrated, Paul's theology is inseparable from the metamythical world-picture of his time.[59] The

56. See Troy W. Martin, "Paul's Pneumatological Statements and Ancient Medical Texts," in *The New Testament and Early Christian Literature in Greco-Roman Context: Studies in Honor of David E. Aune*, ed. John Fotopoulos (Leiden: Brill, 2010), 102–23.

57. Paula Fredriksen, *Paul: The Pagans' Apostle* (New Haven: Yale University Press, 2017), 158.

58. Thiessen, *Paul and the Gentile Problem*, 140–43; David Bentley Hart, "Postscript to the Paperback Edition," in *The New Testament: A Translation* (New Haven: Yale University Press, 2017), 593.

59. David Bentley Hart uses the term "metamythical" to describe the way Jakob Böhme and "gnostic" sects like the Valentinians or Sethians tend toward "mythopoeic

texts of the biblical anthology "speak in a strange language with concepts from a distant time, from a strange world-picture." They do not speak directly to or for communities of faith today. In order for them to become meaningful, "they must be *translated*"—that is, we must recontextualize their ideas in terms of a contemporary world-picture and cosmic imaginary.[60]

How might we hear Paul's claim "I have been crucified with Christ" shorn of his ancient assumption that, by participating in the rite of baptism, a person is penetrated and permeated by the substance of *pneuma*? After the sect of Jesus followers awaiting the end of history became the Christian religion seeking stability and permanence, the subsequent ecclesiastical tradition made two routes, both of which abandon Paul's apocalyptic context, the main options within theology. On the one hand, the particularist approach is to sacramentalize this ancient practice by retaining the importance of the baptismal rite while dematerializing *pneuma* as a kind of spectral reward one receives for one's participation in the church. But this leaves us with the unsatisfactory result that the church institution becomes the exclusive dispenser of divine grace—whether for adults, who participate consciously, or for infants, who participate unconsciously (though at the conscious resolve of their parents). Either way, a soteriological ecclesiocentrism binds divine mercy to the church—thereby also implicitly endorsing the violent history of coloniality as the divinely ordained process of spreading redemption to the otherwise *massa damnata*. On the other hand, the traditional universalist approach is to metaphysicalize Paul by replacing *pneuma* with a universal substance—a cosmic *humanum*, or human nature—that suppos-

exorbitances." Such could also be said for Paul himself, who breathed a similar air in the ancient Mediterranean world. See David Bentley Hart, "The Modern Invention of an Ancient System," *Leaves in the Wind*, September 9, 2021, https://davidbentleyhart .substack.com/p/the-modern-invention-of-an-ancient.

60. Rudolf Bultmann, "Ist voraussetzungslose Exegese möglich? [1957]," in *Glauben und Verstehen: Gesammelte Aufsätze*, 4 vols. (Tübingen: Mohr, 1933–1965), 3:142–50, at 145.

edly unites every person who has ever lived, and which God assumed in the incarnation. According to this view, salvation occurs, in principle, independently of any individual person's existence. In the Eastern tradition, salvation occurs primarily in the "marvelous exchange" of the incarnation itself, whereas Barth, in the Western Protestant tradition, adapts this account to his crucicentric Protestant theology of election and justification. In the Western church, especially, it has been customary to view the metaphysical exchange of properties as a potentiality that must be fully actualized by the individual's conscious act of faith or participation in the sacramental institution of the church.

Existential universalism proposes an alternative to these two routes that abandons both the metaphysical *humanum* and the sacramental ecclesiocentrism: the former because it lacks the existential dimension and requires some kind of mythical cosmology and ontology; and the latter because it objectifies the divine act of salvation as a possession of the church, disregarding the eschatological understanding of salvation as God's decisive action. What is needed is an account of salvation that is concretely related to each person without requiring their conscious participation or the mediation of the church. Both conscious participation and ecclesial mediation limit the overflow of divine grace to the achievement of certain finite conditions, thereby effectively rendering the human more powerful than God—as if God were somehow obstructed by finitude. Conscious participation constrains God at the individual level, while ecclesial mediation constrains God at the communal level. Both are sheer impossibilities if God is the utterly transcendent ground of existence, the eschatological power of the future underlying all reality. The only theologically credible account of salvation is therefore one that is both individual and unconscious. This rules out the classical interpretation that claims God acts upon the primary substance of the general *humanum* and thereby supposedly affects each individual; such an account, while attractive in certain respects, is not meaningfully related to the individual and assumes an ontology that is largely incredible to people today. Armed instead with Bonhoeffer's account of unconscious Christianity and Ellacuría's notion of the crucified people, I propose to translate Paul's story of cocrucifixion into an existential framework. One advantage of this approach is that it closely approximates the existentially disruptive and socially revolutionary character of early Christian apocalypticism, albeit without requiring the belief in a literal apocalypse supposedly arriving in the imminent future—a belief that the ongoing course of history quickly proved false.

As a starting point, we can begin by affirming Paul's soteriological presupposition that *pistis* enables one to receive the *pneuma* of Christ—and with subjective soteriologies, we can affirm that this reception of *pneuma* is the event of reconciliation itself. There are three components here that require unpacking: *pistis*, *pneuma*, and the mode of reception. I have already reconstructed the idea of *pistis* as *fides directa*—an unconscious faith, a passive receptivity to the action of God. To borrow from Eberhard Jüngel, such faith is "a most lively, most intensive, indeed most *creative passivity.*"[61] The *pneuma* poses a special challenge. Post-Nicene readers of the New Testament have tended to quickly identify *pneuma* with the Holy Spirit, the third person of the trinity, but this interpretive decision cuts short our ability to hear what Paul is actually saying. The *pneuma* is not a divine hypostasis but an astral substance—indeed, the very substance of the resurrected Christ, who has gone through the process of astralization ahead of us and risen to join the celestial beings in the starry host. To receive this material into one's body is quite literally to have Christ "live in me." The *pneuma* thus represents Christ himself; it is the

61. Eberhard Jüngel, "Der menschliche Mensch: Die Bedeutung der reformatorischen Unterscheidung der Person von ihren Werken für das Selbstverständnis des neuzeitlichen Menschen [1988]," in *Wertlose Wahrheit: Zur Identität und Relevanz des christlichen Glaubens—Theologische Erörterungen III* (Munich: Kaiser, 1990), 194–213, at 212.

extension of his glorified, post-Easter reality to the individual person. For us today, then, to "receive the *pneuma*/spirit" means to share, in some way, in Christ—to enjoy a connection between our existence and his. Paul assumed the connection was material; medieval orthodoxy assumed the connection was metaphysical; here I will assume the connection is existential, a reality that occurs in the act of existing itself.[62]

The question to ask at this point is this: Who (and what) is Christ, theologically speaking? What constitutes the theological meaning of his existence such that we can speak of a connection between his existence and ours, a sharing of our being in his? For those theological ontologies that assume, whether implicitly or explicitly, that being is something prior to and separate from action, the answer could be "the glorified *pneuma* that we receive in baptism" (in the mythical cosmology of the ancient Mediterranean) or "the human essence that substantially unites all people and that Christ assumed in the incarnation" (in the Neoplatonic cosmology of late antiquity and beyond). All such world-pictures and conceptualities are inessential to the event itself, and thus we are free to replace old interpretive models with new ones. An existential approach, by contrast, does not assume the priority of

62. Implicit here is a dispute with the traditional doctrine of the trinity. Most Christian theologies, including theologies of universal salvation, have assumed as a given that any genuine Christian theology must conform to the Niceno-Constantinopolitan doctrine of the trinity, but this doctrine represents such a departure from the intellectual world of the early community of Christ followers that it might as well represent a different religion altogether. If we abandon, as I believe we should, any notion of orthodoxy as constraining what must be said theologically, then we ought to be free to develop theologies that reconstruct an account of Christianity without the later assumptions of ecclesiastical orthodoxy, not in a misguided effort to retrieve some pure Christian faith—there is no original "true Christianity" to recover—but because seeing these texts without the blinders of later dogma can open up theological pathways that hold promise for contemporary spiritual life. While it is entirely possible to develop an existential universalism within a trinitarian grammar (I did so in *The God Who Saves*), abandoning this grammar, and the metaphysics of the Godhead that it presupposes, makes better sense of the New Testament texts in light of the latest historical research. To be sure, new constructions will be necessary in the next generation, but someone needs to take the initial step.

being to action but instead lets the action of Christ determine the nature of his being. Theologically speaking, Christ is not some substance, material or immaterial, but rather a mode of exist= ing. According to the apostle Paul, the existence in question is a *crucified* existence (1 Cor. 2:2). This is why Paul understands the saving relationship between Christ and himself in terms of cocru- cifixion. He must be crucified with Christ in order to participate in the justifying consequences of this event. To be sure, this is not a literal cocrucifixion (there are no nails or wooden beams here), which raises the question, What does it mean for a person to be metaphorically crucified? We gain insight into the answer from Paul's statement "It is no longer I who live" (Gal. 2:20).

Paul's claim "It is no longer I who live" is presented as a matter of fact, as something already definitively accomplished, and yet it has no experiential anchor or empirical verification, nor could it. Even if one did believe in a material *pneuma* infused into a person in baptism, this would have to be believed against appearances, *sub contrario specie*, as Luther says regarding the theology of the cross—that is to say, *sub specie crucis*. The event of cocruci- fixion is thus an event that gives a person no security, nothing to hold on to as a guarantee. There is nothing here to possess; it is instead the event of our dispossession. Our life is no longer ours. It is now Christ who lives in our place. Moreover, the cocrucify- ing event in which Christ now lives in us is the very event of our resurrection. The apostle Paul states elsewhere that "if Christ is in you," this means that the one "who raised Christ Jesus from the dead will give life to your mortal bodies through the indwelling of his *pneuma* in you" (Rom. 8:10–11, my trans.). Paul draws a direct connection between the resurrection of the Christ and the indwelling of Christ's *pneuma* in each person, but the latter is also how Paul understands cocrucifixion: the crucifixion of our self in baptism, whereby we receive the infusion of the messianic *pneuma*. In other words, cocrucifixion and coresurrection occur simultaneously. Just as cocrucifixion is a present, existential event, so too is our resurrection; it is not deferred to the chronological future but happens now insofar as we share in the pneumatic reality of the Christ. The paradox of this event reinforces the point that there is no new possession here but only constant dispossession. Indeed, Paul declares the truth that "Christ lives in me" in the absence of any proof—in the very *absence* of Christ. There is indeed a double absence here: not only is Christ not present to us in any self-evident manner (i.e., Christ does not relieve us of the burden of continuing to live our lives), but now, in this act of cocrucifixion, we are no longer present to ourselves (i.e., "It is no longer I who live"). Paul suggests that our salvation consists precisely in the correspondence between our existential absence and the absence of the Crucified One. If Christ is the one who experiences the fathomless depths of God-abandonment, then we participate in Christ precisely in those moments in which we enter into the abyss of our existential estrangement, into the mystery of God's presence-in-absence. In this experience of absence—or rather, in this nonexperience of presence—we correspond to the crucified Christ himself.[63]

All of which is to say that salvation, in this sense of the term, occurs in the death of the existential self-understanding by which one seeks to be in full possession of oneself, by which one claims to be fully present and to have this presence in hand. This self-understanding is what Luther, developing an Augustinian insight, understood as humanity "curved in upon itself" (*incurvatum in se*).[64] Those who are curved in upon themselves are those who insist on securing their identities from all interruption. Insofar as many religious and spiritual programs promise to give each person a stable life of purpose, fulfillment, and blessed assurance, they serve only to increase one's existential incurvature. Salvation, in

---

63. In my book *The God Who Saves*, I develop this further by exploring the cry of dereliction in the Gospel of Mark.

64. Martin Luther, *Martin Luthers Werke: Kritische Gesamtausgabe*, 73 vols. (Weimar: Böhlau, 1883–2009), 56:356.5. Hereafter cited as *WA*.

the existential sense that Paul describes, is thus a salvation *from* precisely these efforts of self-help and self-fortification.

Whereas Christians traditionally speak of being saved from eternal death or the final judgment, an existential universalism says instead that we are saved *from ourselves*—from the illusion that we belong to ourselves, from the anxious attempt to secure our identity and freedom, from the insatiable desire to be in full possession of ourselves and our future. Our participation in Christ's death, wherever and however this occurs—consciously or unconsciously—involves the death of our self (i.e., our old self-understanding), while our corresponding participation in his resurrection involves a new creation (i.e., a new self-understanding) that traditional language describes as freedom from our enslavement to sin. This new self-understanding is not a new form of security, one in which *I* come to life again. On the contrary, the I, the ego, remains dead, supplanted by the Christ who lives in me. This is another way of saying, to borrow again from Luther, that to be saved is to be *placed outside ourselves*. As Luther wrote in his 1531 lectures on Galatians, "our theology is sure, because it places us outside ourselves."[65] Luther captures the paradox not only of theology but of existential salvation itself: the certainty or assurance that it provides comes only in the very removal of certainty and assurance, through the act of our existential displacement. To be placed outside ourselves does not mean we are securely relocated elsewhere, just as "Christ living in me" does not mean Christ is now our personal possession who does our living for us. The saving act is an ongoing *displacing*, and "Christ living in me" is a permanent *removing* of the self. Such is the alienness of divine grace; it remains alien even as we become participants in it.

The above, while existentially framed, is largely a restatement of the traditional Protestant account of salvation as *iustitia aliena*. But the traditional picture assumes certain conditions—namely,

65. WA 40.1:589.8.

the explicit proclamation of the gospel, particularly in word and sacrament, and the conscious response of faith. Many are willing to embrace an existential account of salvation so long as the sole context for this salvation is a distinctively religious ceremony that reinforces the necessity of the institutional church, thereby making the church the exclusive provider of spiritual goods and services. Shorn of such assumptions, we can fully entertain the possibilities opened up by Bonhoeffer's concept of unconscious Christianity.

We can begin by asking, Where do we experience being placed outside ourselves? When do we find ourselves displaced? The answers to these questions are going to be particular for each person, which is precisely why this is an existential soteriology; but these are also going to be questions that every person can answer, which is why this is a form of universalism. Many experience this displacement in aesthetic encounters with works of art— novels, films, poems, plays, paintings, and concerts. Others have this experience in practical encounters, such as creating a work of art or perfecting a craft, or in collaborating with others on long-term projects of value and significance. Others are placed outside themselves in erotic encounters, when the sensuous experience of another body draws one out of one's ego in a moment of ecstasy (*ek-stasis*, lit. "standing outside oneself"). Still others are displaced in ethical encounters with those in need, whether caring for a child or pet, helping a friend or neighbor, or responding to the needs of a stranger. We can multiply such potential sites of displacement ad infinitum. The point is that, regardless of the context, there are "fleeting instants scattered throughout our lives when all at once, our defenses momentarily relaxed, we find ourselves brought to a pause by a sudden unanticipated sense of the utter uncanniness of the reality we inhabit. . . . When it comes, it is a moment of alienation from the ordinary."[66] This

66. David Bentley Hart, *The Experience of God: Being, Consciousness, Bliss* (New Haven: Yale University Press, 2013), 88.

moment of alienation from the ordinary is an alienation from our old selves—so much so that, in this fleeting instant, "it is no longer I who live."

Salvation as Existence

In *Diversity and Identity*, his 2001 essay on theological anthropology, Ian McFarland proposes a novel account of what constitutes theological personhood—his term for what I call salvation.[67] To avoid setting up a single attribute all must share or a single pattern to which all must conform, strategies that inevitably leave some people out or violently erase their experience, McFarland argues that personhood is constituted not by any quality possessed by the human person but instead by the act of being addressed by God in Jesus, "quite apart from how we may respond to that address."[68] This act of address has no more definite content than the fact that it is "good news." What this good news looks like in each case will depend on the person being addressed by Jesus, since Jesus's own identity is bound up with "the bewildering diversity of characters (including both the dead and the not yet born) from which his own particular identity as a person cannot be separated."[69] Moreover, McFarland draws on texts like Matthew 25 to argue that "if we want to encounter Jesus, it is the other whom we need to meet, because it is as we encounter the other that we encounter Jesus."[70]

This implies, not only that the gospel address by Jesus *cannot* be limited to the ecclesial space of explicit proclamation and confession, but also that we in fact encounter this address primarily in

67. McFarland explicitly makes the connection between these terms. Regarding Aquinas, he writes, "Thomas argues that . . . [Christ's] headship is the cause rather than the consequence of our salvation (and thus, in the language of the present essay, of our personhood)." Ian A. McFarland, *Difference and Identity: A Theological Anthropology* (Cleveland: Pilgrim, 2001), 56.
68. McFarland, *Difference and Identity*, 23.
69. McFarland, *Difference and Identity*, 20, 24.
70. McFarland, *Difference and Identity*, 23.

the complex messiness of everyday existence. And the "we" here is everyone. This vision is by no means limited to a select few who alone are truly persons. As McFarland makes clear, the doctrine of the *imago Dei* suggested by this account of personhood does not establish "a model to which individual beings may or may not conform" but instead functions "as a lens through which individuals can be perceived as persons."[71] In other words, the point of McFarland's doctrine of theological personhood is not to provide a rubric by which to discern who is a person and who is not. Everyone is already a person, and this account provides Christians a way to understand why on theological grounds, thus hopefully helping them to see each person *as* a person. The same is true for universalism, particularly existential universalism. Everyone is already saved, and this account aims to provide Christians with a way to understand why—not because this is something each person needs to understand about themselves (far from it!), but because Christians need to see each person as saved and not as an object of their conversion and ministry. *It is Christians who need a doctrine of universal salvation.* All humans, as well as all nonhuman animals and the rest of the creaturely order, are already, and repeatedly, the recipients of God's boundless grace; they need nothing from the Christian community.

The politics of existential universalism also becomes clear precisely at this point. So much of what makes for political life is a matter of visibility and invisibility: Who is visible to the brokers of power, and who is invisible? Someone may be visible *as a person*—recognized as a significant member of society, worthy of participating in the structures of social and political power. But someone else may be visible *as a nonperson*—recognized only as someone to be disciplined and policed by the power structures. Such an individual is visible within these structures only as an object and not as a subject, and is thus practically invisible. The

71. McFarland, *Difference and Identity*, 22.

account of existential universalism put forward here addresses this
situation in two ways. First, it acknowledges that everyone who
experiences the existential dislocation of life (i.e., everyone) is a
recipient of divine grace and thus a person in the full theological
sense of that term. In this regard, those who are consciously Christian are called outside of themselves to see the others in their midst
in their true humanity. Christianity, as a religious practice, is an
act of *seeing* those who are denied visibility in society. Second,
because existential universalism understands salvation as the unconscious experience of the absence of God—as the existential
participation in Christ's crucifixion—it sees those who have been
disenfranchised and invisibilized in society as the truest recipients
of God's presence, the primary sites of God's revelation breaking
into history. Salvation belongs most authentically to them, and
the purpose of conscious Christianity is to call Christians back
to their unconscious faith in solidarity with all of humanity and
the rest of creation.

No doubt some will find this approach to soteriology unsatisfy-
ing. Those who expect salvation to involve righting the wrongs of
human history will be disappointed, but this was always asking
too much of religion. It is also the wrong request. People like to
think that their all-powerful deity could sort out history's competing claims for recompense through some cosmic act of repara-
tions, but few stop to consider what such an eschatology would
require. Most people who harbor such a vision of the beyond have
little interest in universalism; they expect their god not only to
bestow infinite blessings on them but to punish their enemies with
everlasting torment. And, more than likely, those enemies pray to
a deity who will supposedly accomplish the reverse. We are left
with the heavenly mirror image of the violent factions on earth,
with each party convinced that their god is the true one who will
figure everything out. But this is a crude image of the divine. Ex-
pecting God to swoop in as history's deus ex machina to fix what
humankind has messed up assumes a Santa Claus deity that is little

more than the projection of our unfulfilled wishes for justice. In the face of the world's injustice, the purpose of religion is not to promise that everything will be fine someday in the ever-receding future but rather to provide solace to those in grief, sustenance for those in need of inner replenishment, and stimulation for those seeking to rectify injustices. While every theology ought to be emancipatory in its aims, what those seeking emancipation need is usually not a promise of eschatological wish-fulfillment but a community of people ready to get to work. The task of righting history's wrongs is not God's work but ours.

For those who simply want a universalism that maintains a more traditional account of postmortem salvation and future redemption, one need look no further than the other chapters in this volume. But some will likely not want existential universalism to be an option because they see something insidious in the theology proposed here. Because of its lack of an afterlife or cosmic renewal, some may charge existential universalism with undercutting any motivation for evangelism—or even for being Christian at all. To such charges I can only plead guilty. There are few ideas more distinctively Christian than the assumption that our theologies ought to reinforce our own rightness in practicing this particular religion, whether through apologetic efforts to "prove" the truth of our doctrines or kerygmatic efforts to scare people into conversion by proclaiming the ungodly terrors that await them if they should fail to say a magical prayer or participate in an enchanted ritual. The moment a theologian comes along and announces this to be a bunch of immoral hogwash, they are lambasted for destroying any rationale for faith. Which is truly a remarkable admission. The implication is that no one would be a Christian if they were not forced into it, either intellectually or emotionally—or, in the case of colonialism, physically. Christians who are invested in the evangelistic spread of their religion would do well to think long and hard about where this anxiety comes from and what it says about the god they claim to believe in. When any theology that does not support the agenda of ever-increasing church growth and missionary expansion is treated as a threat to the faith, it is hard not to conclude that said faith is less of a gospel and more of a grift—a spiritual multi-level marketing scheme.[72]

In the face of charges that universalism undermines evangelism, many theologians have gone on the defense and sought to show how universal salvation supports evangelism by giving Christians a better message: one rooted in love and grace, rather than fear and hellfire. To be sure, saying that everyone should be a Christian because Christianity has good news to share is a significant improvement upon saying that everyone should be a Christian because anyone who is not a Christian will burn in hell. But that is like saying sitting in a timeshare pitch meeting is superior to being waterboarded in a black ops prison. No one would deny it, but who would thereby conclude that the former was the best of all possible scenarios? The problem with most Christian theologies of salvation is not merely that they use threats to compel belief but the underlying assumption that compelling people to join the church is necessary and good, that all people would be better off if they were Christian. There is a certain arrogance internal to so much Christian theology, whether universalist or nonuniversalist, because of the assumption that people are saved by Christ alone and that acknowledging this will somehow improve our lives, either because it will rescue us from eternal torment in the afterlife or because it will provide joy in our present lives. The former is monstrous, and the latter is a self-help program, a weekly meeting in which we hear some advice for healthy,

<hr>

72. Cryptocurrency might be an even better analogy here. Ahshuwah Hawthorne, a former pastor from Hawaii who now works with evangelical bitcoiners, "said he thought of Bitcoin as a primer for religion: Both required evangelizing, conversion, and community building. And both required acceptance of a higher power you cannot control: just like you can't rewrite the Bible, you can't change the rules of bitcoin." See Emily Shugerman, "'We're a Cult': Inside Bitcoin's Shameless Hypefest," The Daily Beast, April 11, 2022, https://www.thedailybeast.com/inside-the-bitcoin-2022-conference-in-miami-beach.

happy living and are assured that Jesus has paid for our heavenly timeshare.

Existential universalism, by contrast, is not an argument for why people should become or stay Christian; that is entirely for each person to decide. It is not even an argument for how people are saved. Ultimately, I propose, we are saved by our very existence, by our experience as animals encountering the wonder of life and the mystery of being connected to the rest of the cosmos. The purpose of the theological and biblical argument is simply to point to this by drawing upon the sources and norms that characterize the Christian faith. Existential universalism gives people who are already followers of Jesus, who simply know themselves to be Christians and need no rationale to justify this, a lens by which to understand all others as recipients of God's saving presence. Existential universalism does not claim to be the only right approach to Christian theology—and that is precisely the point. Maybe if our theologies were less invested in being right, to the exclusion of alternatives, we might actually get closer to the gospel.

About the Contributors

David W. Congdon is Senior Editor at the University Press of Kansas, where he acquires in the fields of political science, law, US history, Indigenous studies, environmental studies, and religion. He is also adjunct instructor at the University of Dubuque Theological Seminary and Colgate Rochester Crozer Divinity School. He is the author of *The Mission of Demythologizing: Rudolf Bultmann's Dialectical Theology* (Fortress, 2015), *Rudolf Bultmann: A Companion to His Theology* (Cascade Books, 2015), *The God Who Saves: A Dogmatic Sketch* (Cascade Books, 2016), and *Who Is a True Christian? Contesting Religious Identity in American Culture* (Cambridge University Press, 2024).

Tom Greggs, FRSE, holds the Marischal Chair of Divinity at the University of Aberdeen, where he also served until recently as Head of Divinity. A Methodist theologian, he serves on the World Council of Churches Faith and Order Commission. His recent books include *The Church in a World of Religions: Working Papers in Theology* (T&T Clark, 2022); *Barth and Bonhoeffer as Contributors to a Post-liberal Ecclesiology: Essays of Hope for a Fallen and Complex World* (T&T Clark, 2021); *The Breadth of Salvation: Rediscovering the Fullness of God's Saving Work* (Baker Academic,

2020); and *Dogmatic Ecclesiology*, vol. 1, *The Priestly Catholicity of the Church* (Baker Academic, 2019). He is currently working on the second volume of his trilogy on ecclesiology.

Morwenna Ludlow is Professor of Christian History and Theology at the University of Exeter. She is a priest in the Church of England and holds an honorary position as Canon Theologian at Exeter Cathedral. Her academic research has focused on the fourth-century theologian Gregory of Nyssa and on early Christian use of rhetoric. She is the author of *Universal Salvation: Eschatology in the Thought of Gregory of Nyssa and Karl Rahner* (Clarendon, 2000) and *The Early Church* (Tauris, 2008), an introduction to the first few centuries of Christian history and theology.

Robin A. Parry is an Anglican priest in the diocese of Worcester, UK, and an editor for Wipf & Stock Publishers. He is the author of *The Evangelical Universalist* (Cascade Books, 2006, 2012), under the pseudonym Gregory MacDonald, and various other works on Christian universalism.

Scripture Index

Subject Index

accommodation, 66
activism, 69–73
afterlife
  and cognitive science, 128–31
  and existential universalism, 136,
    161–62
  feminist critique of, xix–xx
  history of, 131–33
  immanent, 147
  patristic understanding of, 5, 27, 30–31
  as rebirth, 132
  theological arguments against, 133–35
aiōnios, 67
Allin, Thomas, 49n42, 63–64
Ambrose of Milan, 16
Ambrosiaster, 16
angels
  education by, 27
  fallen, 4, 18–19, 22, 77
  and *pneuma*, 148–49
animism, 132
annihilationism, xviii, 34, 37, 46, 49, 56
anonymous Christianity, xiv
anthropology, 131–33
  theological, 23–25, 138–39, 158–59
Apocalypse of Peter, 13
apocalypticism, 149–50, 152

apokatastasis, xvii, 18, 27, 141
  Barth's rejection of, 81, 82n6, 104–5
Aquinas, Thomas, xiv, 136, 158n67
Arminianism, xvii, xxi, 34, 57–59,
    64–65, 76
asceticism, 5, 27–28
astralization. *See* resurrection
atonement
  and the cross, 144
  penal substitution, 74, 75n97, 101–2
  ransom theory of, 16
  and the Spirit, 123
  universal, 47, 59
Augustine of Hippo, 86

Ballou, Hosea, 46–47, 75n97, 75n98
Balthasar, Hans Urs von, xv, 13, 22,
    81–82, 100n57, 143
baptism, 73, 138–39, 149–50, 153–54
Barclay, William, 49n42
Barth, Karl, xii–xiv, 81–124
  actualism of, 106–7, 118–19
  on the afterlife, 133–35
  and Berkouwer, response to, 108–12
  on condemnation as impossible pos-
    sibility, 98
  and election, xii–xiii, 85–96, 98

169

Hades, 15–16
harrowing of hell, 12–16
Hart, David Bentley, xviii–xix, xxii,
    145–46, 149n59, 157
heaven, 24, 128
hell, xvii, xix, 34, 37–38, 70n84, 71n90,
    75, 82, 98
  eternality of, 49, 55, 59, 67n79
  and scripture, 62, 64, 67, 78
  See also afterlife; harrowing of hell
Hellbound? (2012), xviii, 50
heresy, 36–38, 46
Hick, John, xv–xvi, xxii, xxviiin31,
    141–42
Hilary of Poitiers, 16
Hodge, K. Mitch, 130–32
Holy Spirit, 53, 152
  and Barth, 121–23, 121n125
  necessity of, 59, 63
  See also *pneuma*
humanity
  addressed by Jesus, 158–59
  being in Christ, 102, 139–40
  curved in upon itself (*incurvatum in
    se*), 155
  and *enhypostasis*, 113
  and intersectionality, 145
  as mediator, 23–24
  as microcosm of the universe, 24
  nature of, 24, 28, 150
  temporal limitation of, 134–35
  union of, with Christ, 43
  See also election; freedom: human
humanum, 150–51
Hunsinger, George, 83n7, 102
Huntingdon, Joseph, 47

image of God (*imago Dei*), 68, 93, 146
immortality, xix–xx, 129–31, 133–35
incarnation, 7, 19, 24, 52, 151, 153
  church as prolongation of, 146

inclusivism, 76
intertextuality, 7–8, 11

Jesus Christ
  absence of, 155, 160
  election of, 85, 87–92, 95–97, 100–
    101, 106–7, 109, 112–14, 120, 123
  history of, 111
  mediating work of, 53, 87, 96
  resurrection of, 52, 54–55, 93–95,
    101–2, 116, 143, 154, 156
  as revelation, 12, 52, 84, 87
  as subject matter of theology, 84,
    103, 110
  victory of, 103, 111–12, 115–16
Johnston, Sarah Iles, 133
Judas Iscariot, 88n19, 95, 98n53
judgment, 26, 35, 67, 75, 86, 91–93, 96,
    118, 156
Jukes, Andrew, 49, 61, 65–67, 72n92
Jüngel, Eberhard, 133–35, 152
justification, 35, 96, 136, 151

Law, William, 43
Leade, Jane, 39, 43n26
liberation theology, xvi, 144–47
Luther, Martin, 118, 154–56

MacDonald, George, xiin1, 49n42,
    72n92
MacDonald, Gregory, xviii–xix, 50
Macrina the Younger, 21, 28–29
Marlowe, Frank, 132
Martin, Troy, 148–49
Maury, Pierre, 85
Maximus the Confessor, 22–25
McClymond, Michael J., xixn21, 127n6
McDowell, John C., 122n130
McFarland, Ian A., 158–59
mission
  of God, 22, 56
  purpose of salvation, 73, 77